*Charleston Gardens and the
Landscape Legacy of Loutrel Briggs*

Charleston Gardens

and the Landscape Legacy
of Loutrel Briggs

James R. Cothran

The University of South Carolina Press

© 2010 University of South Carolina

Published by the University of South Carolina Press
Columbia, South Carolina 29208

www.sc.edu/uscpress

Manufactured in China

19 18 17 16 15 14 13 12 11 10   10 9 8 7 6 5 4 3 2 1

LIBRARY OF CONGRESS CATALOGING-IN-PUBLICATION DATA

Cothran, James R., 1940–
    Charleston gardens and the landscape legacy of Loutrel Briggs /
James R. Cothran.
        p. cm.
    Includes bibliographical references and index.
    ISBN 978-1-57003-891-4 (cloth : alk. paper)
    1. Briggs, Loutrel Winslow, 1893–1977. 2. Landscape architects—
South Carolina—Charleston—Biography. 3. Landscape architecture—
South Carolina—Charleston—History. 1. Title.
    SB469.385.S6C68 2010
    712.092—DC22
    [B]   2009042204

Frontispiece: *Camellia japonica*
Page v: A garden on Church Street, Charleston

Dedicated to Charleston gardeners, both past and present,
who have opened their garden gates and invited visitors
to step inside and enjoy the beauty of the gardens within

Loutrel Briggs will live in our memory, in our hearts, and in the gardens he designed as long as we honor his work by our care and maintenance of them, in our city, our state, and beyond.

Mrs. Sallie Carrington-Chaney, president
of the Garden Club of Charleston, 1977

Contents

Illustrations

Preface

Although Loutrel Briggs designed a wide range of projects, including parks, church grounds, college campuses, cemeteries, and estates, he is best known for the many small gardens he designed in Charleston, South Carolina, beginning in 1929 and continuing to 1977. Briggs is credited with designing more than one hundred small gardens in the city's historic district alone. While many of these gardens have survived, others have been lost because of destruction, redesign, or woeful neglect. Today Charleston is in grave danger of losing one of its most precious and most enviable assets—its legacy of "Briggs Gardens."

The purpose of this book is twofold: to create a greater awareness of landscape architect Loutrel Briggs (1893–1977) and his contributions to Charleston's landscape legacy and to provide information associated with the preservation of significant Briggs gardens through the use of archival resources and garden easements. While the focus of the book is on Charleston gardens and their preservation, the information is applicable to other cities, towns, and locations as well.

Charleston has a long and enviable reputation for preserving its architectural treasures through preservation efforts and building easements. Now is the time for the city to become a leader in landscape preservation through the promotion of garden easements. This objective can be achieved through public education and establishment of a comprehensive garden-easement program. As with building easements, financial incentives are available for the establishment of garden easements, as historic preservation specialist Eric Reisman explains in appendix 1 of this book. Charleston is in an enviable position of serving as a model for other communities to follow in ensuring that gardens, like buildings, are preserved as an important part of America's heritage.

Acknowledgments

I would like to express my appreciation to the following individuals, organizations, and agencies that played an important role in making *Charleston Gardens and the Landscape Legacy of Loutrel Briggs* possible. First and foremost I would like to thank landscape architect David Utterback for his stewardship and donation of Loutrel Briggs' archives to the South Carolina Historical Society in Charleston, South Carolina. This extensive collection of Briggs' plans and drawings includes a wide range of projects completed during a landscape-architectural practice that lasted fifty-six years.

The second individual I would like to express my appreciation to is Karen Prewitt of Charleston, South Carolina. Following the donation of Briggs' archives to the South Carolina Historical Society, Karen played a central role in cataloging and processing the collection. This time-consuming task facilitated access to Briggs' work for study and research. Karen continues to serve as a strong advocate for the protection and preservation of Briggs' gardens and landscapes.

I also wish to recognize the professional assistance of Pat Kruger for genealogical research on Loutrel Briggs. This effort uncovered important details of Briggs' life, education, and career. I also thank Barbara Orsolits for conducting and recording numerous oral interviews with individuals who knew or worked with Briggs during the time he lived and practiced landscape architecture in Charleston and the region. Special recognition also goes to Eric Reisman for his comprehensive analysis and discussion of garden easements, which is included in this book as appendix 1.

I would like to thank and recognize the following individuals (both living and deceased) for sharing their experiences, memories, and personal recollections of various aspects of the life and career of Loutrel Briggs. While the following list is in no way complete, it includes some of the many individuals who assisted in compiling material for this work: Mrs. Emily Whaley; Mrs. William Coleman; Mrs. Robert Whitelaw; Mrs. F. W. Farr; Elise Pinckney; Clermont Lee; Marty Whaley Cornwell; Patti and Peter McGee; Mary Martha Blalock; Jan McDougal; Janet Tantum; Craig Bennett, Sr.; Sallie Carrington-Chaney; Jimmy Small; Robert Marvin; Billy and Mary Hills; Robert Cuthbert IV; Mrs. Elizabeth Verner Hamilton; Hugh and Mary Palmer Dargan; Susan Epstein; Nancy Hoel; Martha Severens; Laura Vardell; Helen Goforth; Jonathan Poston; James Reap; April Wood; Karen Emmons; Dan Krall; John Sherrer; Jane Thornhill; W. R. and Eudora Roebling; Arthur Schirmer, Jr.; Ed and Nan Lawton; Warren Ripley; Blake A. Bell; Elizabeth Bradham; and René Shoemaker. Each of these individuals, as well as others, played an important role in helping to document Loutrel Briggs' life and career.

Special recognition also goes to the capable and accommodating staffs of the South Carolina Historical Society, Historic Charleston Foundation, the Charleston Library Society, the Charleston Preservation Society, the Charleston County Public Library, the Charleston Museum, the Caroliniana Library at the University of South Carolina, the Cherokee Garden Library of the Atlanta History Center, the Charleston Garden Club, the Garden Club of South Carolina, Parsons the

New School for Design, and the Carl A. Kroch Library of Cornell University.

Sincere appreciation is also extended to the production team who provided support in the preparation of text, editing, and illustration of this publication. Foremost among these are Sarah McElmurray for her patience and perseverance in typing the manuscript, along with its many changes and modifications. Mary Ann Eaddy did a superb job in the review of the text and recommended editorial changes, while Janet Barrickman contributed to the support and production of important components of the publication. Max Birnkammer also provided invaluable assistance with the production of visual images used in the book.

Finally there are others too numerous to mention who played an important and meaningful role in the research, documentation, and production of this work. They are to be thanked for their support, assistance, and encouragement in making this book possible.

Charleston Gardens and the
Landscape Legacy of Loutrel Briggs

Trumpet vine and hummingbirds, from John James Audubon's *Birds of America*

OFTEN DESCRIBED AS "a city set in a garden," Charleston, South Carolina, has a rich garden tradition dating back to colonial times. Charleston became the center of gardening in the southern colonies, and some of the country's finest houses and gardens were built outside the city along the Ashley and Cooper rivers. Planters who had acquired their wealth in the Carolinas and the West Indies developed these large estates, known as plantations. Prominent among these were Crowfield, Middleton Place, Drayton Hall, and Magnolia on the Ashley; along with Mulberry, Medway, and Middleburg on the Cooper. Fine houses and gardens were by no means confined to plantations outside Charleston but were equally prominent in the city, where they were the homes of wealthy merchants and traders. Plans of many of Charleston's early town gardens have been preserved through property-transfer records in documents known as the McCrady Plat Books. In almost every instance, these early town gardens were laid out in simple geometric patterns of square and rectangular designs.

Shortly after the American Revolution, houses built in Charleston began to depart from the established colonial designs to a vernacular style known as the "single house." This long, rectangular, freestanding structure was specifically designed for Charleston's long, narrow lots and semitropical climate. The single house was typically built with its gable end facing the street and its rooms strung out in a straight line in order to obtain maximum use of space. A variety of outbuildings—including slave quarters, detached kitchen, stables, well, and privy—were located at the rear of the property. The single house featured porches, known locally as piazzas, that extended the entire length of the house on the south or west side. In late afternoon and evening, piazzas caught the cool, refreshing ocean breezes and became delightful outdoor living spaces. An outer door that opened onto the piazza traditionally overlooked a small, patterned garden whose design was based on a combination of geometric shapes including circles, squares, and rectangles.

The destructive effects of the Civil War (1861–65) had a tremendous impact on Charleston's plantations and city gardens. Many of Charleston's finest plantations, including Middleton and Magnolia, suffered tremendous damage and destruction, and the city's town gardens were greatly impacted as well. Shortly after the war, a northern reporter described Charleston as "a city of ruins, of desolation, of vacant houses, of widowed women, of rotting wharves, of deserted warehouses, of weed-filled gardens, of miles of grass grown streets, of acres of pitiful and voiceful barrenness." Charlestonians found themselves in a state of poverty with little in the way of financial resources to rebuild their homes or maintain their gardens.

Charleston suffered for many years under what has been appropriately described as genteel poverty, a situation that afforded few opportunities for gardening or the pursuit of horticultural interests. This no doubt accounts for the observation by Frances Duncan in *Century Magazine*

Middleton Place, Charleston, South Carolina. Of the more than seventy plantations that once existed along the Ashley and Cooper rivers, one of the finest was Middleton Place, developed by Henry Middleton circa 1741. Conceived in a bold and expansive manner, the garden includes grassy terraces, butterfly lakes, groves of trees, formal walks, alleys, and a canal.

(March 1907) that few gardens in Charleston, South Carolina, conformed to Victorian gardening styles or followed principles of informal design espoused by Andrew Jackson Downing, America's first professional landscape gardener: "Rarely is the serenity of a Charleston garden marred by 'bedding out' by tightly packed beds of violently diverse colors. . . . Nor is the 'landscape garden' often among those present; that is, the garden which concerns itself chiefly with green lawns and informal shrubbery."

It was not until the early 1900s that economic conditions improved and a renewed interest in

Charleston's town gardens began to emerge. Perhaps because of limited financial resources or simply because professional garden designers were unavailable during this time, Charleston gardeners relied on their own talents to fashion many small, creative town gardens. In the 1920s and 1930s, tourists began to visit Charleston, not only to see the gardens at Magnolia and Middleton plantations but also to experience the wonderful display of springtime flowers in the city's charming town gardens during the peak blooming season that lasts from mid-February to mid-April. While most of Charleston's town gardens were

A view of Charleston in the early 1900s

A typical Charleston single house with piazzas and patterned garden

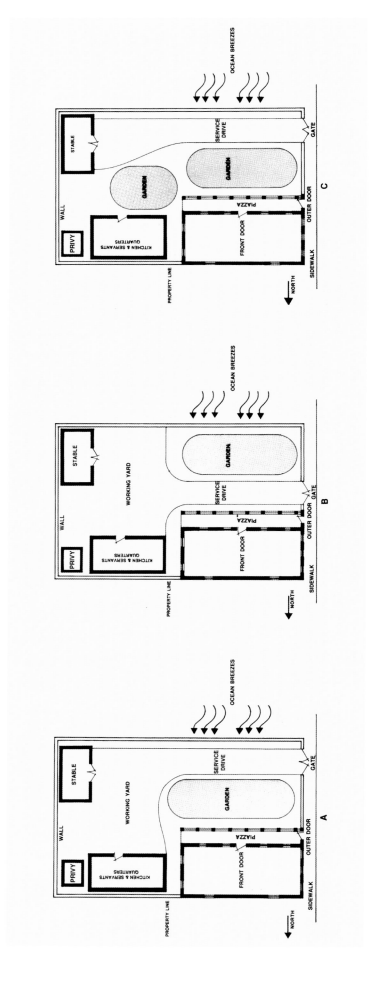

Plans A and B depict typical layouts of Charleston houses and gardens. Plan C shows an expansion of the side garden to the rear of the property. This transition occurred during the early part of the twentieth century as the need for service yards gradually disappeared.

Located on the lower end of King Street, just around the corner from White Point Garden, this small city garden was originally designed by Briggs in 1951 for Mr. and Mrs. Lloyd Willcox.

contemporary in design, they reflected traditions from the past by virtue of their historic setting and wealth of details—high brick walls, iron gates, spacious piazzas, cobblestone walks, and a myriad of eighteenth- and nineteenth-century architectural details. Many of these new gardens were expanded to the rear of the house into areas that had originally accommodated a variety of outbuildings and a work yard.

The design of Charleston's small town gardens reached a state of refinement under the professional influence of landscape architect Loutrel Briggs (1893–1977). The gardens Briggs designed in Charleston throughout his career are appropriate to the climate, architecture, historic setting, and lifestyle of the city. Briggs' gardens reflect a wonderful sense of scale, combining house and garden into a unified whole. While these gardens are secluded and private, at the same time they are an integral part of the overall

urban fabric of the city. Much of their charm and appeal is achieved through the limited views they afford from the street through wrought-iron gates, as well as the visual benefits they derive from surrounding vistas of church spires, colorful tiled roofs, picturesque buildings, and ancient walls of neighboring gardens. Briggs' gardens may best be described as a total sensory experience. Within their intimate boundaries one perceives the element of age and appropriate sense of scale, experiences the sensitive use of historic materials, smells the perfume of flowers and the fragrances of sweet-scented shrubs, hears the sound of distant chimes of church bells, and enjoys the occasional sense of silence captured within a totally private world. Loutrel Briggs, above all others, is credited with establishing "Charleston's Garden Style," a design style that has gained national and international recognition and acclaim.

Chapter Two

Biographical Profile of Loutrel Briggs

LOUTREL WINSLOW BRIGGS was born December 12, 1893, in New York City to Frank Elwood Briggs and Ella DeMarsan Loutrel Briggs. Briggs' father, a native of Maine, graduated from Haverford College in 1883 and served as auditor of the freight division of the New York Central Railroad. Briggs' mother was born in New York and grew up in Manhattan, where she was active throughout her life in charitable work associated with "crippled children, and the aged/infirm."

Briggs, an only child, lived with his parents during his formative years. After completing New York's Trinity Preparatory School, he enrolled in the prestigious Art Students League of New York. Located in the Fine Arts Building on Fifty-seventh Street, the art school was founded in 1875 and graduated such notable artists as Frederic Remington, Winslow Homer, Alexander Calder, Isamu Noguchi, Norman Rockwell, and Georgia O'Keeffe. Following a year of study at the Art Students League, Briggs abandoned his paints and brushes to pursue a career in landscape architecture.

To pursue this interest, Briggs enrolled in the Outdoor Art Program at Cornell University in Ithaca, New York, in 1914. Begun in the late 1890s, the program offered a variety of courses in English, chemistry, biology, botany, physics, geology, political science, history, surveying, and drawing, along with classes in landscape design, plant materials, engineering, and architecture.

Briggs proved an able and talented student. The university still retains samples of his academic work in its archives, ranging from the designs of estates in Connecticut and New York to a university master plan. All these projects received the honor of "1st Mention." Not only are the design solutions exceptional for a college-level student, but the renderings exhibit Briggs' artistic skills, no doubt acquired from his earlier training as a student at the Art Students League of New York.

While attending Cornell, Briggs worked during the summer on a farm outside Stamford, Connecticut, where he gained experience in growing fruit trees and general farm practices. Briggs obtained a leave of absence from Cornell for military service from March through June in 1917. During that time he served as inspector for the French Commission in the United States at Eddystone, Pennsylvania.

Briggs graduated from Cornell in 1917 with a degree in landscape architecture. It is believed (although undocumented) that following graduation Briggs apprenticed in the office of a landscape architect—a practice promoted by the university as a means of gaining hands-on experience. Graduates were also encouraged, if possible, to broaden their design skills through domestic and foreign travel. Following several years of apprenticeship, Briggs opened an independent practice of landscape architecture in New York City in 1921. That same year, he was elected a member of the Architectural League of New York. Established in 1881, the organization was initially formed to promote architecture, then later painting, sculpture, landscape architecture, and industrial art. Beginning in 1886, the Architectural League initiated an annual exhibition, allowing

View of the Cornell University campus, circa 1916

A representative project Briggs completed while a student at Cornell

Loutrel Winslow Briggs at age twenty-four

Catalog for the New York School of Fine and Applied Art, 1927–29, with locations in New York, Paris, and Italy

its members to display examples of their work as well as providing the public an opportunity to stay in touch with progress in the arts. Throughout his career Briggs entered examples of his work in the Architectural League's annual exhibition.

While building his practice, Briggs became an instructor of landscape architecture at the New York School of Fine and Applied Art in 1924. He was appointed head of the Department of Landscape Architecture in 1926 and taught classes in landscape architecture and garden design until 1929.

The program included three years of study focusing on landscape architecture and garden design. Courses were directed at developing knowledge of the principles of landscape design and the methods of their application through lectures and drafting, accompanied by a wide range of academic projects. Classes were also offered in "interior architecture and decoration," thus enabling the student to treat the house and grounds as a single composition. Academic study was enhanced by trips to parks, botanical gardens, and private estates. The third year of study included one term in Paris, accompanied by lectures and organized trips to gardens in Italy, France, and England. Today the school is known as Parsons the New School of Design, named in honor of Frank Alvah Parsons (1866–1930), who was instrumental in influencing design education in America.

In an interview conducted by Rowena Wilson Tobias for the February 23, 1941, issue of *Charleston News and Courier,* Briggs revealed that initially he was somewhat intimidated by teaching "as he much preferred to use the abstractions of blueprints and a drawing pencil to convey his ideas." He soon overcame the difficulty of lecturing and began using his newly developed speaking skills outside the classroom to give presentations to garden clubs and civic organizations—a practice that he continued throughout his professional career.

While Briggs was teaching at the New York School of Fine and Applied Art, his students participated in a national design competition that was open to all U.S. schools and colleges teaching landscape architecture. Briggs' students' submission won first place, and as a reward for this achievement, the students were offered a study tour of European gardens. In 1924 Briggs and twelve students set out for a three-month tour of gardens in Italy, France, and England. This experience, no doubt, left a lasting impression on the students as well as Briggs, who felt that the opportunity to visit, study, and photograph European gardens provided him "a clearer understanding of what could be achieved with American gardens." On returning to the United States, Briggs used the experience of his travels to give public lectures on European gardens to the Metropolitan Museum of Art, the International Garden Club, the Horticultural Society of New York, and other organizations in the region.

Throughout Briggs' tenure at the New York School of Fine and Applied Art (1924–29), he maintained an independent practice of landscape architecture. The combination of a part-time practice conducted in concert with an academic position was not uncommon for young professionals until they could attract enough clients to support a full-time practice. Briggs left his teaching position in 1929 to devote all his time and energies to landscape architecture. His one-man business continued to grow with an increasing number of projects ranging from parks, estates, subdivisions, schools, college campuses, cemeteries, and private residences. Examples of his work include Woodside Park, Stamford, Connecticut; Fella Park, Essex Falls, New Jersey; Lynncraft Terrace subdivision, New Rochelle, New York; Grand View subdivision, Pleasantville, New York, and Gipsy Trail Club, Carmel, New York—along with a number of private estates and gardens.

A pivotal point in Briggs' professional career occurred when he visited Charleston, South

Above and overleaf: These illustrations from *Italian Gardens* (1907), by George Elgood, suggest the type of gardens Briggs and his students visited in 1924.

Carolina, in 1927 at the age of thirty-four. Whether it was prompted by a desire to experience Charleston's springtime beauty and historic charm or to evaluate the potential for future work from the many wealthy northerners who were purchasing properties in Charleston and the Carolina lowcountry as winter retreats, Briggs' visit led to his decision to open a seasonal office in Charleston in 1929. This was the beginning of his system of practicing landscape architecture in the North during the summer and in Charleston during the winter. Briggs generally resided in New York from May to October, and in Charleston from early November to April.

When Briggs first opened his office in Charleston, the profession of landscape architecture was a relatively new field. Most professionally trained landscape architects were located in large metropolitan areas such as Boston, New York, and Philadelphia. Except for several projects undertaken in Charleston by the New York landscape architectural firm of Innocenti and Webel, the area was a prime market for a talented landscape architect. While Briggs' earliest projects in Charleston were for northern clients, he soon began to receive commissions from local residents who recognized his expertise as a talented designer. By tradition Charlestonians (overlooking sectionalism and memories of the past) readily embraced outsiders who possessed unusual design talents and exhibited a sincere appreciation of the city's cultural and historic past. Briggs met each of these criteria.

In addition to seeing future business opportunities in Charleston, Briggs may also have been drawn to the area through his acquaintance with Emily Crompton Barker (1887–1950), the daughter of William C. Barker and Sarah D. Crompton of Philadelphia. Emily moved to Charleston in the mid-1920s, and in 1927 she was employed as manager of Mrs. Jack Brantley's studio on Church Street. In 1928 Emily opened an interior design and antiques shop on the ground floor of 77 Church Street (a three-story structure) next door to the Brewton Inn at 79 Church Street,

A typical walled Charleston garden

Vista through garden toward
wrought-iron gateway

ABOVE all else, these old Charleston gardens have a marvelous sense of seclusion and privacy. There is also a perfect mergence of house and garden; between these two, it is out in the garden that one reads, plays bridge, sews or has tea inevitably—and invariably. The close proximity of the garden to the house is, of course, what gives this intimate quality, while the wonderful walls—architecturally speaking, the chief glory of the gardens—insure the absolute privacy. These walls are usually solid and seven or eight feet high, so that from the street the only glimpse of the garden is through an exquisite wrought-iron gate, swung between great gateposts, as illustrated here.

Gateway to
Stoney House
by moonlight

Article in the May 1926 issue of *Woman's Home Companion*. Throughout the 1920s many national magazines promoted Charleston as a tourist destination. The city was renowned for its mild winter climate, historic architecture, and charming walled gardens.

Back Road to Pipersville, by Fern Coppedge (1883–1951). Artists were drawn to Bucks County, Pennsylvania, because of the area's picturesque landscapes, historic farmhouses, stone walls, and quaint villages.

where Briggs resided during his early visits to the city. Whether their first meeting was by chance or arranged by mutual friends, Emily and Loutrel's love of Charleston and the charm of its historic architecture and gardens appears to have played an important role in solidifying their relationship, eventually leading to their marriage in 1929.

Following their marriage, the couple lived in Charleston during the winter months on the upper floors of 77 Church Street above Emily's shop. Emily was a member of the Garden Club of Charleston and was active in the Charleston branch of the English Speaking Union (ESU). During World War II, she served as a staff assistant for the Red Cross, both in Charleston and Philadelphia. Throughout their marriage Loutrel

and Emily maintained a summer home, known as Pennstone, in Doylestown, Pennsylvania, the seat of Bucks County, which became an important center of creative expression in the visual and literary arts during the 1920s. The natural beauty of the Pennsylvania countryside, along with its close proximity to Philadelphia and New York, helped the area develop into a well-known artist community. While many of the visual artists who settled in Bucks County had roots in Philadelphia, most of the writers and theater people came from New York.

While records indicate that Loutrel Briggs was actively involved in numerous landscape projects in Doylestown and the surrounding area, including design of the grounds of the Bucks County Historical Society, little is known of his possible

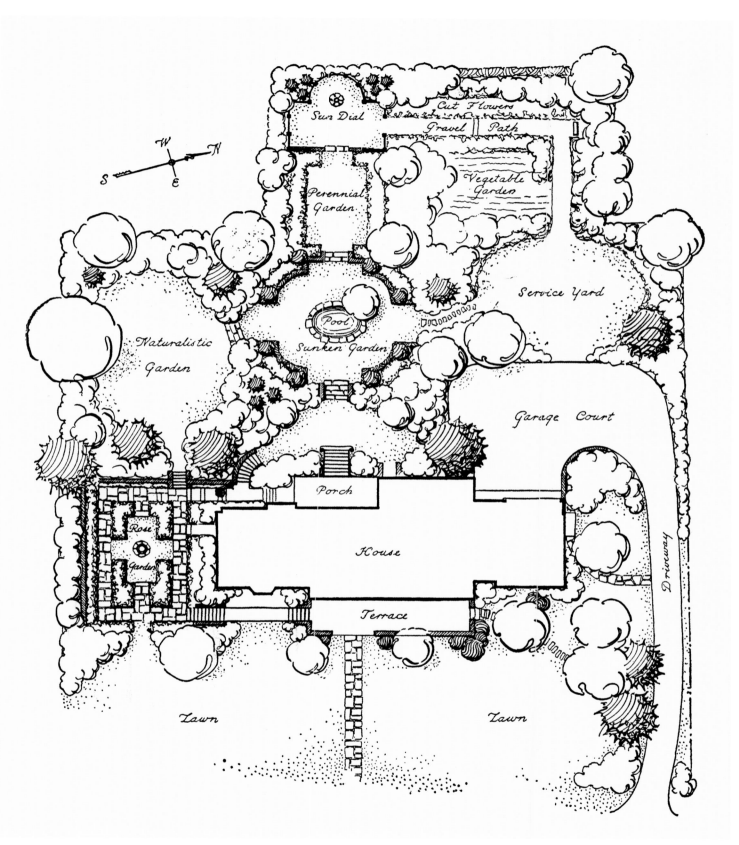

Plan of the residence and garden of Mr. George M. Waugh, Jr., in Scarsdale, New York, as illustrated in the February 1932 issue of *House Beautiful* magazine. The accompanying article notes that the landscape plan was prepared by Briggs and Carl Stelling "with admirable effort despite the difficult terrain." The lower levels of the property were developed into attractive gardens of various designs.

The brick wall flagstone court is shaded by a fine old Oak (opposite page). The dependencies have been made into garages with a chauffeur's apartment and additional maids' rooms

Garden Plan

ARCHITECTURE, JUNE 1936   47

Plan and landscape features of the Washington Roebling garden, from the June 1936 issue of *American Architect and Architecture*

After purchasing the William Gibbes House in 1928, Mrs. Roebling commissioned Briggs to design the grounds. She was eager to create a new garden for the property but was insistent that its design be in keeping with the spirit of the past. To accomplish this objective, Briggs developed a design that respected the historic integrity of the site and reflected the tradition of old Charleston gardens. Articles about the garden appeared in the January 15, 1933, issue of *Town and Country* magazine, the March 1933 issue of *House and Garden,* the January 1936 issue of *House Beautiful,* and the June 1936 issue of the *American Architect and Architecture.* Each of these lavishly illustrated articles displayed Briggs' talent for garden design.

By 1933 Briggs' one-man office had expanded to the point that he invited Carl Stelling of New York to become a partner in the firm—thence to be known as Briggs & Stelling. Stelling received his early landscape-architectural training abroad and later studied at Stevens Institute of Technology, located on the Hudson River across from midtown Manhattan. Shortly after joining Briggs, Stelling became engaged to Helen Greeff of New York City. She graduated from the Brearley School, attended Smith College, and was a senior at Barnard College at the time of the engagement.

During the six years that the partnership lasted between Loutrel Briggs and Carl Stelling, the firm completed many commercial, municipal, and residential projects in New York, Pennsylvania, Massachusetts, and Connecticut. The New York office of Briggs and Stelling was initially located at 10 East Fortieth Street and later at 101 Park Avenue. In addition to numerous projects in the Northeast, a steady flow of projects were also carried out in Charleston (no doubt under the supervision of Briggs during the winter months), including town gardens, plantations, and several public-housing projects.

Whether the relationship between Briggs and Stelling deteriorated over time because of business or professional differences or was impacted by Mr. Stelling's divorce from his wife, Helen, in

involvement in the Bucks County artist community. No doubt he and Emily simply enjoyed the area for its natural beauty and the opportunity to partake of the many local cultural activities.

One of Loutrel Briggs' first design commissions in Charleston was for Mrs. Washington (Cornelia) Roebling, widow of the famous engineer Washington Augustus Roebling, who oversaw the construction of the Brooklyn Bridge. Shortly after the death of her husband, Cornelia Roebling, a native South Carolinian, purchased the William Gibbes House, located at 64 South Battery. This handsome Georgian structure was built in 1772 by William Gibbes, a wealthy merchant-planter.

1939, the partnership was dissolved that same year. As noted in the *New York Times* (June 22, 1939): "The firm of Briggs and Stelling . . . has been dissolved and the members Loutrel W. Briggs and A. Carl Stelling will continue the same line of business as individuals." Following the dissolution of the partnership, Briggs operated as a one-man firm until several years before his death, during which time David Utterback served as an associate in Briggs' Charleston office.

Briggs often presented lectures and study programs on a variety of landscape subjects to civic and community groups. As early as 1931, Briggs offered a short course for Charleston gardeners at the Brewton Inn, covering general principles of garden design, identification of southern plants, and southern plants for winter effect. He also conducted a field lecture on plants in Charleston gardens. *Garden Lectures by Loutrel W. Briggs,* a promotional pamphlet from a later date, offered a series of landscape lectures to garden clubs in the North and the South. The pamphlet lists a range of topics, lecture schedules, and associated fees:

GARDEN LECTURES
by
Loutrel W. Briggs
Landscape Architect

I. THE A.B.C. OF GARDEN DESIGN
Illustrated with slides
The fundamentals of garden design
applied to all types of garden.

Briggs' frequent lectures on southern gardens and flora emphasized plants grown in Charleston gardens, including the camellia (*Camellia japonica*), a traditional favorite.

The South Carolina Memorial Garden, designed by Briggs in 1946

2. GARDENS OF EUROPE
Illustrated with slides
Emphasizing styles and period in garden
art and their relation to gardens today.

3. PLANTS AND PLANTING
Illustrated with blackboard drawings
A practical talk on how, when,
and where to plant.

4. SOUTHERN GARDENS AND FLORA
Illustrated with slides

SCHEDULE
Lecture period for Northern Garden
Clubs from March 15 to October 15
(Traveling expenses from New York Office).
Lecture period for Southern Garden Clubs from

November 1st to April (Traveling expenses
from Charleston Office).

FEES
One lecture: $50.00
Two lecture course: $85.00
Three lecture course: $125.00
Four lecture course: $150.00
Traveling expenses additional, lantern
and operator to be supplied by the club.

Briggs gave freely of his time and talents to
assist with a variety of civic projects, many of
which were sponsored by the Charleston Garden
Club and the Garden Club of South Carolina.
Representative projects include Charleston's Gateway Walk, the restoration of several of historic
Charleston gardens, and the design of the South

Carolina Memorial Garden in Columbia, South Carolina, to honor those who served in World War II. Briggs was also active in Charleston's historic preservation community, serving as a member of the Society for the Preservation of Old Dwellings and a trustee of the Historic Charleston Foundation.

Briggs was active in the American Society of Landscape Architects (ASLA) throughout his career, becoming a member in 1924. Several projects designed by Briggs in the North and the South were included in the 1931, 1932, and 1933 editions of the ASLA publication *Illustrations of Work of Members.* Among them were "The Garden of Mrs. Washington Roebling" at 64 South Battery and "The Courtyard of the Residence of Mr. and Mrs. Loutrel Briggs" at 77 Church Street in Charleston. Other prominent landscape architects whose work was featured in these same publications included Earle Draper, Beatrix Farrand, Charles Gillette, Rose Greely, Ralph Griswold, Arthur Shurcliff, Fletcher Steele and the Olmsted brothers. Through his active participation in ASLA, Briggs was selected as one of two delegates to represent the organization at the International Conference of Landscape Architects held in London in 1948. Following the conference, Briggs traveled for three months throughout England and Scandinavia, studying various aspects of city and urban planning, including design of street patterns, traffic circulation, parks, playgrounds, and housing developments. Briggs later served as chairman of the ASLA Committee for International Relations.

In 1942 the Carolina Art Association honored Briggs by sponsoring an exhibition at Charleston's Gibbes Art Gallery of some thirty of his drawings, photographs, and renderings of gardens. Projects displayed in the exhibit included courtyard gardens; Mrs. Roebling's garden; the garden of Mr. and Mrs. Frederick Richards, Jr.; plans for Mulberry, Mepkin, and Rice Hope plantations; and Charleston's Gateway Walk. The exhibition also included a series of Briggs' measured drawings documenting several eighteenth- and nineteenth-century Charleston gardens.

The year 1950 brought personal sorrow to Briggs with the death of his wife on September 18, at their summer home in Doylestown, Pennsylvania. The couple had enjoyed a happy and successful marriage but had never had children. Emily Briggs was buried in her parents' family plot at Fernwood Cemetery in Philadelphia. As a tribute to his wife, Briggs dedicated his forthcoming book, *Charleston Gardens,* "to the memory of my wife, Emily Crompton Barker Briggs, who first showed me the gardens of Charleston." Published in 1951 by the University of South Carolina Press, the book is a lasting memorial to the mutual love Loutrel and Emily shared for Charleston gardens.

Shortly after opening a seasonal office in Charleston in 1929, Briggs became active in the Charleston branch of the English Speaking Union (ESU), an organization established in 1918 to promote "international friendship through the use of the English language." While serving as president of the Charleston branch of the ESU in 1951, Briggs traveled for two months in the spring of that year through England, Wales, and Scotland under the auspices of the organization. On returning from Europe, he presented a lecture of his travels to members of the Charleston branch of the ESU at the Fort Sumter Hotel.

On June 7, 1953, Loutrel Briggs married Mrs. Virginia Crowe Burks (1895–1989) at Grace Church in Stroudsburg, Pennsylvania. Mrs. Burks was the daughter of Charles Hooper Crowe, writer and lecturer and a descendant of General Zebulon Pike, who discovered Pikes Peak. Prior to their marriage, Virginia Burks, a native of Pennsylvania, resided on Wadmalaw Island, located approximately twenty minutes outside Charleston. She had studied art at the Sorbonne in Paris and spent a number of years traveling in Asia and Europe. She had an interest in gardening and painting, and her artistic training included the study of ceramics at Penland School of Crafts in North Carolina. Mrs. Burks had one daughter, Janet Burks (Tantum), by her first husband, Horace Burks, who was a career naval officer.

Mrs. Washington Roebling's garden at 64 South Battery and the courtyard of the residence of Mr. and Mrs. Loutrel Briggs at 77 Church Street in Charleston, South Carolina, represent two examples of Briggs' work exhibited at the Gibbes Art Gallery in 1942.

Throughout the mid- and late 1950s Loutrel Briggs went through the process of phasing out his New York office to become a full-time resident of Charleston. In 1954, during the transition process, Briggs built a home in Princeton, New Jersey, at 12 Newlin Road and opened a part-time office at 10 Nassau Street in downtown Princeton. It is interesting to note that Briggs' home in Princeton was designed by J. Floyd Yewell, the noted architect and artist who prepared a rendering of the Washington Roebling garden in 1930. Briggs maintained a seasonal home and office in Princeton for five years before becoming a full-time resident of Charleston in 1959. Before that time, Loutrel and Virginia Briggs lived at 71-B East Bay Street for several years and then at 28-A Lamboll. In 1958 Briggs purchased property at 3 Ladson Street in Charleston's historic district,

where he built a permanent residence. The lot on which the residence was constructed contained a small coach house, which Briggs converted into an office. It was from this location that Briggs continued his practice of landscape architecture for the remainder of his career.

In 1962 Briggs built a summer home in Cashiers, North Carolina. The site Briggs selected for his mountain home was located off Wade Road, within walking distance of the High Hampton Inn and Country Club. Many of Briggs' neighbors in Cashiers were Charleston natives who were either friends or former clients. Included among these were the Hagoods, Staats, Rivers, and Pelzers. Like Highlands and Flat Rock, North Carolina, Cashiers was a popular summer retreat for Charlestonians who sought the cool mountain air as a means of escaping the

Briggs' 1951 lecture to the Charleston branch of the English Speaking Union included accounts of his visit to notable gardens in England, Wales, and Scotland. These images from *Some English Gardens* (1905), by George Elgood and Gertrude Jekyll, suggest the type of gardens he saw.

The house at 3 Ladson Street, Charleston, that Briggs built in 1958. At the rear of the property was a small coach house, which Briggs converted into his office.

summer heat and high humidity of the Carolina lowcountry.

During summer trips to Cashiers, Briggs occasionally enrolled in painting classes offered by visiting artists at High Hampton Inn. His continued interest in art is evident in Christmas greeting cards featuring pen-and-ink sketches he did of local Charleston scenes. Briggs painted a number of landscapes that are owned by a private collector in Charleston. His artistic skills are also evidenced in the pencil sketches employed in many of his landscape drawings to convey design concepts. Briggs' garden plans also demonstrate his artistic eye and his ability to create landscapes that in themselves are works of art.

Both before and after Briggs settled in Charleston in 1959, he collaborated on many projects with the Charleston-based architectural firm of Albert Simons and Samuel Lapham. From 1920 to 1972 this highly respected firm served as a leader in Charleston's historic-preservation movement. Simons and Lapham frequently retained Briggs for landscape-architectural services associated with plantations, college campuses, residential sites, and historic-restoration projects. Briggs is also credited with the design of Samuel Lapham's own garden at 4 Greenhill Street in Charleston's historic district.

For eighteen years after making Charleston his year-round home, Briggs continued to practice landscape architecture in Charleston, primarily focusing on garden design. During that time he developed many unique and imaginative designs. Ownership of a Briggs garden became a Charleston tradition, and many native Charlestonians, as well as newcomers, were eager to employ his services. Within Charleston's historic district alone, Briggs designed more than one hundred small gardens, many of which are treasured today for their beauty and individual charm.

In 1960 Briggs was honored for the second time with an exhibition of samples of his works by the Carolina Art Association at the Gibbes Art Gallery. The exhibition, which was held January 3–29, featured nineteen drawings and paintings of his projects in South Carolina, New York, and New Jersey, ranging from courtyard gardens to school grounds. The exhibition reflected a broad spectrum of projects both in the North and South, designed by Briggs during the course of his prolific career. Projects displayed in this exhibition included:

Courtyard garden, Charleston, S.C.
Drawings for gate and garden, Rice Hope, Cooper River, S.C.
School grounds, Pelham, N.Y.
Pool garden, Welawiben, Oakland, N.J.
Garden, Pelham Manor, N.Y.
Garden of Remembrance, Grace Church, Charleston, S.C.
Garden, Spuyten Duyvil, New York City

City garden, 47 Legare Street, Charleston, S.C.

Gate, entrance court, and terrace garden, Mulberry, Oakley, S.C.

Circular garden, Mulberry, Oakley, S.C.

Planting, pool garden at Mepkin, Cooper River, S.C.

Gardens at Mepkin, Cooper River, S.C.

Entrance court and gardens, Bedford Hills, N.Y.

Garden court, 64 South Battery, Charleston, S.C.

Garden, 64 South Battery, Charleston, S.C.

Planting, pool in garden, 64 South Battery, Charleston, S.C.

Shelter and rose garden, 64 South Battery, Charleston, S.C.

City garden, 100 Tradd Street, Charleston, S.C.

Plan for Sunset Memorial Park, Fairview, N.Y.

In describing Briggs, both friends and associates characterized him as a talented landscape architect who always sought to meet the needs and expectations of his clients. Briggs was soft-spoken and reserved, a sensitive individual who seldom shared aspects of his personal life. Briggs' shy and retiring nature was often in sharp contrast to the more outgoing and gregarious personalities of his southern clients. In physical terms Briggs was slight of build, of medium height, and a dapper dresser—always wearing a coat and tie no matter what the occasion or event. Even though he exhibited a restrained and serious nature, he was recognized and highly respected by all who knew or worked with him and was greatly admired for his professional skills, design talents, and contributions to the field of landscape architecture.

Even though Briggs operated primarily as a one-man firm throughout most of his career, he completed a tremendous number of projects of various types and designs. During a period of declining health in the 1970s, he continued to practice landscape architecture primarily in Charleston. He died at his home at 3 Ladson Street on May 20, 1977. Briggs' cremated remains were interred in Fernwood Cemetery in

A Christmas greeting card by Briggs, a pen-and-ink sketch of St. Philip's Church in Charleston

Philadelphia, next to his first wife, Emily. Loutrel Briggs left a lasting legacy of beauty that he created in his practice of landscape architecture, in his book, *Charleston Gardens,* and above all in establishing what is universally known as "Charleston's Garden Style."

The *Charleston News and Courier* published the following eulogy for Briggs on May 26, 1977:

Born and educated in New York, Loutrel W. Briggs came to Charleston 50 years ago as a winter resident, later living here year-round. He

The Garden of Remembrance at Grace Episcopal Church in Charleston

looked at the city and its environs through the professional eyes of a landscape architect and the appreciative eyes of an artist. He looked at it, too, through the eyes of an admirer of old houses and other structures of architectural significance. His keen perception of the potential for beauty in walled city gardens and open plantation vistas alike was reflected in the many private and public grounds he designed in the Lowcountry.

Well traveled and familiar with achievements in design in other cities both in this country and abroad, Mr. Briggs demonstrated in landscape design, and both in articles and lectures, a continuing concern for preserving the past, improving the present, and planning for an orderly future. His interest in helping protect and restore architectural treasures and his expertise in enhancing the charm of gardens, courtyards and streets will be remembered gratefully by all those saddened by Mr. Briggs recent death at 83.

In a memorial service held at the Joseph Manigault Garden shortly after his death, Mrs. Sallie Carrington-Chaney, president of the Garden Club of Charleston, offered the following remarks:

In honoring Loutrel Winslow Briggs . . . these aspects of his life come to mind:

A Briggs garden in late spring

First, a friendship of fifty years. In the 1920s, Loutrel Briggs brought a letter of introduction to my mother. Shortly thereafter he came to Charleston to work and live.

Second, civic leadership. He cared deeply for this city of his adoption. He was involved, and worked for worthy causes he espoused. . . .

Third, an outstanding landscape architect. Among his earliest work was the small garden at 43 Tradd Street, the spacious grounds of Mulberry Castle, later the Garden Gateway Walk, the Heyward-Washington Garden, the Garden of Remembrance at Grace Church, the South Carolina Memorial Garden in Columbia, to name a few.

He opened the eyes of home owners to what could be done to enhance the areas closest to their homes and hearts. To have a garden designed by Loutrel Briggs is like owning something bearing the English Hallmark, or a piece of silver marked sterling. . . .

Loutrel Briggs will live in our memory, in our hearts, and in the gardens he designed as long as we honor his work by our care and maintenance of them, in our city, our state, and beyond.

Chapter Three

Loutrel Briggs and the Charleston Renaissance

BEGINNING AROUND 1915 and lasting into the early 1940s, Charleston experienced a revival of interest in its cultural and historic past during a period traditionally referred to as the Charleston Renaissance. In "Renaissance Revival: An Enduring Legacy," Stephanie Hunt wrote: "In the early 1900s, when Charleston was still reeling from the Civil War and the resulting blows to the Southern economy, the city was an unlikely crucible for creativity. Poverty replaced the wealth of the former plantation economy, and the golden area of antebellum refinement had lost its sheen. But it was from these shadows, these shambles, that a remarkable group of artists emerged to carry forth Charleston's legacy of beauty and reclaim its destitute landscape."

The impressionistic watercolors of Alice Ravenel Huger Smith (1876–1958), the black and white etchings of Elizabeth O'Neill Verner (1883–1979), the Asian-influenced wood prints of Anna Heyward Taylor (1879–1956), and the prints and paintings of Alfred Hutty (1877–1954) played equally important roles in Charleston's Renaissance movement. While each artist came from a different background and training, they formed a vibrant artist community that was instrumental in defining the city's heritage and in rekindling a new appreciation of the unique physical and visual environment of Charleston's cultural and historic past. As noted by Martha Severens in *The Charleston Renaissance* (1998), "The cultural renewal that was the Charleston Renaissance was critical to the invention of the city as a tourist attraction. Through words, melodies, and pictures, the movement's leaders shaped alluring images of the ancient beautiful city that time had forgotten before it was destroyed." Severens further comments that "nowhere else in the country have artists—whether native born or nationally renown—played a greater role in shaping the destiny of a locale."

In *A Golden Haze of Memory: The Making of Historic Charleston* (2005), Stephanie Yuhl notes that local artists did not

adopt a fortress mentality and isolate themselves from external influence. From the very beginning of the movement they welcomed the leadership and participation of non-Charlestonians, such as John Bennett of Ohio, Hervey Allen of Pittsburgh, Alfred Hutty of Michigan, and Laura Bragg of New Hampshire, who were dedicated to the city's heritage but did not share in it directly. By the late 1920s, as the movement expanded, cultural producers also solicited advice from outside organization, such as the American Institute of Architects (AIA), as well as the financial and moral support of increasing numbers of the new Northern property owners who resided in the city and the surrounding countryside during the winter season. . . . They encouraged outsiders to embrace their city and to propagate the traditions for which it stood. They encouraged all comers to share in their version of the Charleston experience.

Briggs' winter residence and office at 77 Church Street

Previous page: *Herons in a Swamp,* circa 1920, by
Alice Ravenel Huger Smith (watercolor on paper)

When Briggs arrived in Charleston in 1927,
the Charleston Renaissance was well underway.
After opening a seasonal office in Charleston in
1929, Briggs was eager to contribute to Charleston's thriving artistic movement. Charleston
eagerly embraced newcomers with artistic talent
who expressed a love and appreciation of the
city's beauty, tradition, and historic past.

Whether by chance or design, the location of Briggs' first residence and office at 77
Church Street, situated at the corner of Tradd
and Church, placed him in the center of Charleston's artistic community. Anna Heyward Taylor
and Alice Huger Smith lived on Church Street;
Alfred Hutty's studio was on Tradd Street; Elizabeth O'Neill Verner and novelist-playwright
DuBose Heyward (1885–1940) lived and worked

close by. This area remained the center of the
city's artistic movement during and after the
height of the Charleston Renaissance.

Briggs' training as a landscape architect provided him with an appreciation of art, architecture, and design, as well as a sensitivity to the
physical environment. With this impressive set
of skills, Briggs soon made contributions to the
Charleston Renaissance in the articles he wrote
on Charleston gardens and the city's garden traditions. As early as 1930, Briggs wrote an article
for *Country Life* titled "Amateur Gardens—As
Seen by a Landscape Architect." In the article
Briggs provided an interesting analysis of the
work of amateur garden designers and highlighted three Charleston gardens, including those
of Mrs. A. J. Greer, Mrs. J. C. Simonds, and
Elizabeth O'Neill Verner. Briggs considered the
gardens excellent examples of amateur work in a
city known for its long-standing tradition of gardening and horticultural interests.

In describing Mrs. Verner's garden, which
was modeled after a small, walled garden she had
seen in New Orleans in 1925, Briggs offered the
following observations and comments: "Although the smallest and simplest of all, it furnished many fascinating pictures. In spite of a
plot which is shady, crooked and small, it was
not hard for Mrs. Verner to bring into lovely
lines the comparatively few materials used in this
tiny garden. Even the plants offered a difficulty,
for they were all gifts. If you have ever tried to fit
donations from well-meaning friends into a garden and get even approximately the effect you
want, you will appreciate the problem. But, if you
are an artist, the results will be a perfect picture."
Briggs gained invaluable insight into the design
of small-space gardens by observing excellent
examples created by amateur Charleston gardeners. He frequently employed similar spacial
concepts and landscape treatments in his own
designs.

In May 1934 Briggs published "Little Patterned Gardens of Charleston" in *House and Garden,* noting at the beginning of the article:

Partly forgotten in the glamour of the greater gardens around Charleston are a number of smaller, but delightful gardens of old time charm within the city itself. Wandering among its quaint streets one will find here and there a spot where ancient bricks still form pleasing patterns of little beds and narrow winding paths, time honored roses climb and half conceal their trellises, and now and then a proud Camellia displays its perfect blooms. In some, long neglect and sun-denying walls, perchance, have sadly reduced the planting, leaving but a few tenacious survivors bending gracefully over antique gates, or casting somber shadows on well-worn walks, inviting soft green moss, and thoughts of days gone by. Many of these old gardens may easily be seen by the passer-by who pauses by their boundary fences.

The article includes measured drawings and descriptions of five historic gardens that Briggs discovered in his wanderings about the city. While some of the designs were Victorian in nature, others reflected patterns of earlier times. Briggs concluded by noting: "For those who seek beauty brought in years gone by, there is still in Charleston ancient architecture, quaint streets, and mellow gardens."

Briggs' article "Charleston's Famous Gardens" appeared in a special issue of *House and Garden* (March 1939) focused on the architectural treasures and garden heritage of Charleston and the Carolina lowcountry. The issue highlighted significant plantation homes, notable town houses, and the region's wealth of exquisite gardens. Briggs' article provided an overview of Charleston's garden history and horticultural traditions. In the introduction he noted, "Charleston's gardens, which bring so many pilgrims to her gates every spring, are old and new, well tended and neglected, trim and overgrown, formal and casual. It does not matter. One wanders through quaint streets, glimpsing on the one hand emerald lawns, well kept gravel paths and flower borders: on the other an overgrown Camellia bush,

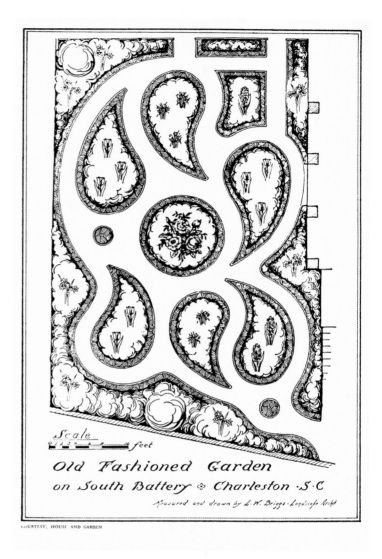

Scale

Old Fashioned Garden on South Battery ⊹ Charleston ·S·C

Plans of eighteenth- and nineteenth-century gardens recorded by Briggs were included in a May 1934 *House and Garden* article titled "Little Patterned Gardens of Charleston." Courtesy of Condé Nast Publications

bits of old brick edging, long-forgotten flower beds, unpruned shrubs and trees. Over both brood the past and the memory of a hundred gardens long gone. For both the neglected and the well-kept are part of the tradition of gardening which has been Charleston's from early times." The article contains descriptions of several old gardens, including the garden at the Sword Gate House, 52 Legare Street; the garden at the Miles Brewton House, 27 King Street;

Old postcard images of Magnolia and Middleton plantation gardens. Briggs featured these gardens in an article titled "Charleston's Famous Gardens," published in the March 1939 issue of *House and Garden*.

Camellia japonica and *Azalea indica*. Briggs' book, *Charleston Gardens* (1951), played an important role in drawing thousands of tourists to Charleston's historic and contemporary gardens, noted for their incomparable springtime display of camellias and azaleas.

and the old geometric garden at the Col. William Rhett House, 54 Hasell Street. Briggs also provided elaborate descriptions of Charleston's world-renowned plantation gardens—Middleton and Magnolia—offering a comparison between formal and informal designs.

Articles about several Charleston gardens Briggs designed for northern clients were published in national magazines, including *Country Life* (1932), *Town and Country* (1933), *House and Garden* (1933), and the *American Architect and Architecture* (1936). These lavishly illustrated articles played an important role in promoting Charleston as a city noted for its historic homes, lovely gardens, and picturesque beauty. Through these contributions Briggs played an important role in helping to promote Charleston as a tourist destination.

Briggs' continued interest and expanding knowledge of Charleston's famous gardens and horticultural heritage, eventually lead to his book, *Charleston Gardens,* published in 1951. Briggs initially proposed the idea of preparing a book on Charleston gardens to the Carolina Art Association in early 1947. In a March 5, 1947, letter to Briggs, Robert Whitelaw, director of the association, indicated an interest in such a book. While discussions of the proposal continued between Briggs and the association, Briggs eventually decided to have the book published by the University of South Carolina Press. In the spring of 1951, the Carolina Art Association sponsored a reception at the Gibbes Art Gallery to promote Briggs' newly published book.

Charleston Gardens contains a wealth of narrative and visual material related to the area's botanical and horticultural heritage, historic and contemporary gardens, plantation landscapes, and ornamental plants. The publication was enhanced with botanical prints, historic and contemporary garden plans, lists of ornamental plants, and black-and-white photographs by Adamson Brown. The cover of *Charleston Gardens* features a rendering of the Washington Roebling garden by the well-known New York architect and artist J. Floyd Yewell (1886–1963), which first appeared in the January 1932 issue of *Country Life* magazine. Not only did *Charleston Gardens* document Charleston's horticultural and garden history, but it also played an important role in drawing thousands of tourists to Charleston

each year to see the incomparable springtime display of azaleas and camellias in city and plantation gardens alike. The book further elevated Briggs' professional standing as an authority on Charleston gardens—both old and new.

Through his diverse skills as a landscape architect, educator, author, and garden historian, Briggs made many contributions to Charleston, both during and after the Charleston Renaissance. From his initial encounter with Charleston in 1927 until his death in 1977, Briggs' love of Charleston was apparent as he sought to inform, educate, and inspire others to experience first-hand Charleston's historic charm and physical beauty.

Chapter Four

Historic Preservation and Urban Planning

CHARLESTON HAS long been recognized for its pioneering efforts in historic preservation, beginning as early as 1920 with the formation of the Society for the Preservation of Old Dwellings, the earliest community-based historic preservation organization in America. The society, now known as the Preservation Society of Charleston, was founded by a dedicated group of individuals to protect and preserve Charleston's architectural treasures. First headed by Miss Susan Pringle Frost, the organization received financial support and professional expertise from local citizens and individuals from outside the city.

Loutrel Briggs became an active member of the Society for the Preservation of Old Dwellings shortly after opening a seasonal office in Charleston in 1929. Desiring to assist the organization in increasing its membership, Briggs realized that, as a newcomer to Charleston, he was in a position to do something native Charlestonians were reluctant or unwilling to do. In "Suggestions for New Comers," published in an early issue of the society's newsletter, Briggs described his approach to recruiting new members: "When entering a local establishment to buy an item or to pay a bill, I would ask the owner if they were a member of the Society for the Preservation of Old Dwellings. The answer I invariably received was 'no.' In response I would say something like this: Do you know that you are getting my trade just because of the fine old buildings here in Charleston, and that they bring in more residents to the

city? I think you should support the organization that is working to preserve them because they bring you business. Only one refused and I have forgotten his name, because I never went back."

One of the first independently executed preservation projects in Charleston was the restoration of Catfish Row, which Briggs carried out in 1928. Located at 89-91 Church Street, the property originally was known as Cabbage Row because of the vegetable stalls located in the area, but it later became known as Catfish Row after DuBose Heyward called it that in his 1925 novel *Porgy.* The structures in Catfish Row consisted of two eighteenth-century brick buildings separated by an arched passageway that extended from Church Street to a T-shaped interior court. The buildings originally accommodated a variety of commercial and residential uses until they fell into disrepair and were finally abandoned in the 1920s. In 1927 the dilapidated buildings attracted the attention of Briggs, who was wintering in Charleston at the Brewton Inn on Church Street, a short distance away.

Briggs' trained eye saw beyond the crumbling walls and sagging roofs of Catfish Row and envisioned the restoration of the property into a revitalized mixed-use development. Briggs purchased the property in 1928 and set out to bring his vision to reality. The 1928 records of the Rotary Club of Charleston note that "Loutrel Briggs had bought Catfish Row on Church Street and urged Charlestonians to recognize the

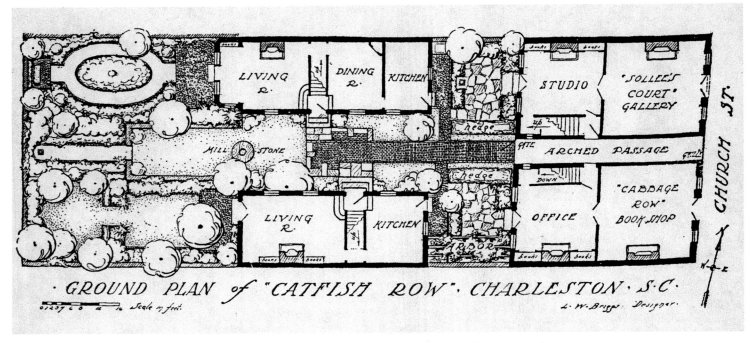

Briggs' restoration plan for Catfish Row, featured in the April 1930 issue of *Country Life*

A view of the interior courtyard that formed the centerpiece of Catfish Row, restored by Briggs in the early 1930s

importance of the preservation of its old buildings and hand-wrought iron work."

Loutrel Briggs' restoration plan for the property was featured in the April 1930 issue of *Country Life* magazine in an article by Eola Willis titled "Catfish Row Comes Back." The article noted that Briggs' design for the property included several retail shops that opened onto Church Street and four residential units that faced an interior courtyard. The residential units were enhanced with a variety of architectural elements, including antique mantels, doors, and hinges rescued from buildings that were being demolished in the area. The interior court was attractively designed to create a gardenlike setting with flowering trees and shrubs, decorative paving, shaded arbors, and other landscape features.

Briggs' restoration of Catfish Row was one of the earliest, if not the first, mixed-use projects in Charleston. When asked if the property's association with Dubose Heyward's *Porgy* had attracted his interest, Briggs answered "no" but that he was "proud of the fact that it was used as the location for the novel." Briggs' pioneering effort in restoring Catfish Row played a significant role in supporting and stimulating community interest in preserving the city's historic resources.

The project did not go without criticism. Several local citizens expressed concern over the "commercialization of Charleston's charm" as evidenced in the restoration of Catfish Row. Briggs responded to these concerns in an editorial in the December 26, 1933, issue of the *Charleston Post and Courier:* "Unfortunately I had been unaware of the harm I had done in restoring the place [Catfish Row], which I found an unoccupied ruin. Many of my neighbors thanked me for cleaning up an eyesore, and I was complimented on saving from destruction a valuable structure of pre-revolutionary design. . . . DuBose Heyward, with an artistry, to which my unskilled pen can not do justice, has preserved for posterity the picturesque life of Catfish Row, and I have attempted to reclaim, with as little external

A present-day view of Catfish Row from Church Street

change as possible to restore the buildings to something of their original state in revolutionary times."

By 1930 Catfish Row had become a viable arts and literary center including such attractions as Sollee's Gallery and the Cabbage Row Book Shop. The upper floors of the complex were leased as artists' studios, offices, and apartments. In 1932 Briggs listed his Charleston office as being located in Catfish Row at 91 Church Street. Records indicate that in 1934 Briggs deeded

Included among the landscape-preservation projects Briggs championed outside Charleston
were the gardens of the historic Hampton-Preston Mansion (left) in Columbia, South
Carolina. Plan by the author based on a 1940 sketch of the original garden plan (above)

Catfish Row to his wife, Emily Barker Briggs, who retained ownership of the property until 1945 when it was sold to Stuart Dawson of Charleston.

Briggs' early preservation efforts in Charleston included the documentation of eightieth- and nineteenth-century gardens he discovered while wandering about the city. In addition to documenting their traditional geometric patterns, Briggs also recorded the plants he found growing within their brick-bordered planting beds. Included among these were old fashioned roses, camellias, sago palms, autumn clematis, plumbago, confederate jasmine, larkspur, periwinkle, violets, and star of Bethlehem. Several of the most interesting gardens documented in Briggs' drawings were those located at 37 Hasell Street, 64 South Battery, 74 Rutledge Avenue, 8 South Battery, and 30 Anson Street. Each of these gardens exhibited a distinctive design. Briggs'

Garden at the Nathaniel Russell House, 51 Meeting Street, whose gardens and grounds Briggs helped restore during his twenty-two years as a trustee of the Historic Charleston Foundation

efforts in identifying and recording eighteenth- and nineteenth-century Charleston gardens was one of the earliest independent efforts by an American landscape architect to document historic gardens.

Not only did Briggs champion preservation projects in Charleston, but he also was engaged in preservation efforts in other areas of the state as well. Of particular note was his support for the preservation of the historic Hampton-Preston gardens in Columbia, South Carolina. Often described as one of the finest antebellum gardens in the South, the Hampton-Preston gardens were well known for their extensive array of box-bordered beds, evergreen alleys, vine-covered arbors, fine sculpture, and large greenhouse filled with unusual and exotic plants. Briggs assisted in raising public awareness of potential destruction of the Hampton-Preston gardens for commercial

development. Speaking to the Palmetto Garden Club in Columbia in 1940, Briggs encouraged restoration of the gardens, noting that the "Hampton-Preston gardens are known as one of the finest historic gardens still in existence. To those interested in history it is a monument." In a presentation to the Columbia Art Association in 1946, Briggs further noted, "In the Hampton-Preston gardens, we have a treasure known to garden lovers all over the Country." Unfortunately Briggs' efforts, along with those of other civic-minded citizens, proved unsuccessful, and the gardens were destroyed in 1947.

In 1947 Charleston's preservation efforts reached an important milestone with the formation of the Historic Charleston Foundation. Incorporated as a not-for-profit organization, the foundation evolved from the pioneering efforts of the Society for the Preservation of Old Dwellings.

50th Festival of Houses & Gardens

CHARLESTON, SC
MARCH 20 – APRIL 19, 1997
Sponsored by Historic Charleston Foundation

The Historic Charleston Foundation's brochure for its 1997 spring tour

Frances Edmunds became the foundation's first executive director and led the organization's preservation efforts and activities for nearly forty years, Many of Historic Charleston's founding trustees had a long history of promoting preservation in Charleston. Included among the nineteen founding trustees were such notable individuals as Loutrel Briggs, Alice Ravenel Huger Smith, Josephine Pinckney, Albert Simons, Henry Staats, Samuel Stoney, Lionel Legge, Ben Scott Whaley, and Robert Whitelaw.

Briggs remained a trustee of the Historic Charleston Foundation for twenty-two years, from 1947 to 1969. During that time he functioned in various capacities, initially serving on the grounds committee, which was formed shortly after the organization was founded. One of the committee's first tasks was to improve the appearance of the gardens of the newly acquired Nathaniel Russell House. Built circa 1808, this house is one of the nation's finest examples of early-nineteenth-century architecture. Briggs was later commissioned to prepare a restoration plan for the garden, including paving details, walks, terraces, and a variety of garden features.

In 1948 the Historic Charleston Foundation initiated the practice of sponsoring annual spring house tours. Tours were traditionally held during the last two weeks of March and the first two weeks in April. Not only were Charleston's town gardens at their finest during this time of year, but Middleton, Magnolia, and Cypress gardens were also at their peak of bloom. In 1951 the fourth annual house tour featured eighteen private homes open for a series of day and evening tours. Visitors were conducted through each home by a knowledgeable hostess familiar with the history and ownership of the property. The purpose of the tours was to generate revenue for the foundation and to educate the public about Charleston's architectural heritage. In 1967 the tour was expanded to include gardens as well. Many of the gardens included on the tours were designed by Briggs.

In 1984 the Historic Charleston Foundation purchased the William Gibbes House, which was

The Cistern and Randolph Hall, College of Charleston. Briggs' desire to develop design and planning solutions that would preserve Charleston's historic character is reflected in his work at the College of Charleston.

threatened by subdivision of its grounds for townhouses or condominiums. The house was later sold by the foundation to a civic-minded individual who donated a conservation easement to the Historic Charleston Foundation, thus protecting the future of the house and preserving the garden, which Briggs' had designed for Mrs. Roebling in 1928 as his first Charleston commission.

In 1987 the Historic Charleston Foundation acquired Mulberry Plantation to protect it from being developed into suburban housing and a golf course. Again the property was sold to a sensitive buyer who enacted the most comprehensive easement restrictions ever received by the foundation. The easement not only addressed preservation of the property's historic house but also provided protection of Briggs' timeless design of Mulberry's gardens and grounds.

Briggs was also a strong proponent of city planning and civic improvement throughout his career. In "Some Reasons for City Planning," which appeared in the December 29, 1948, issue of the *News and Courier,* Briggs offered suggestions on how to "keep Charleston a pleasant place to live." He argued that the proposed construction of a fourteen-story apartment building in Charleston's historic district was in conflict with existing zoning policy and would cause irreparable damage to the historic fabric of the city. Briggs noted that his visits to European cities had helped him to formulate many of his views and opinions on vehicular traffic and urban density—especially in historic cities. In his landscape-architectural practice, Briggs was always diligent in developing design and planning solutions that were respectful of and sympathetic to the city's historic character. This was evident not only in his residential designs but also in his plans for parks, schools, college campuses, institutions, and commercial projects.

In "Landscape Architect's Plea for Roadside Beauty," published in the *News and Courier* on July 25, 1956, Briggs voiced support for local efforts to protect and preserve the historic tree canopy along Highway 17 between Charleston and Summerville, South Carolina:

> The uproar over the oaks on Highway 17 reached me here in Princeton, New Jersey, and I was greatly impressed with the wide interest aroused and with the excellent arguments in defense of the trees. It made me more aware of how dependent the charm of Charleston, which brings me back each fall, is to those who love its gracious way of life and who fight every encroachment on their highly civilized environment. . . . In 1951 I wrote, "Between Charleston and Summerville, formerly a summer resort of the early plantation owners and now famous as the 'Flower Town,' the moss-hung highway is a route of rare beauty and historic interest. Preservation of the roadside as a state parkway would certainly add to Charleston's prestige as a place sincerely proud of its past and sufficiently appreciative of its natural endowments to protect its future."

Briggs' support, no doubt, helped save the oaks on Highway 17 and raised awareness of tree preservation in the Charleston area.

In "A Primer on Urban Redevelopment," which appeared as an editorial in the April 12, 1964, issue of the *News and Courier,* Briggs voiced his opinion regarding urban renewal. He pointed out the failure and negative impact of urban

An aerial view of Charleston's historic district. Briggs frequently championed efforts to preserve and protect Charleston's historic fabric and sense of place.

renewal on homeowners, small businesses, and established neighborhoods. Briggs offered various alternatives to federally funded programs, mentioning several examples of locally funded redevelopment projects successfully carried out with few if any negative consequences. Each of these projects, said Briggs, avoided condemnation proceedings, relocation of families, and disruption of neighborhoods and communities. The articles mentioned in this chapter are just a few examples of Briggs' interest in city planning, civic improvement, and the preservation of Charleston's historic urban fabric.

A tree-lined avenue at Boone Hall Plantation, an example of the lowcountry live-oak avenues
Briggs was a proponent of protecting

THROUGHOUT HIS CAREER Loutrel Briggs gave generously of his time and talents to assist with community and civic projects, many of which were carried out in concert with the Garden Club of Charleston. The following individuals were in attendance at the organization's first meeting in 1922: Mrs. Thomas Pinckney, Mrs. Daniel Ravenel, Mrs. Edwin Parsons, Mrs. D. Porcher, Mrs. C. Norwood Hastie, Mrs. Bessie Ravenel, Mrs. A. J. Greer, Mrs. B. A. Hagood, Miss Constance Frost, and Mrs. Annie L. Sloan. The primary objective of the organization was "to advance gardening in the city." The club's first civic project was the planting and care of the grounds at the Charleston Library Society at 164 King Street in downtown Charleston. Briggs assisted the Garden Club of Charleston with a number of significant projects, including Charleston's Gateway Walk, the Heyward-Washington House garden, and the garden of the Charleston County Free Library, located in the historic Jenkins Mikell House on Rutledge Avenue from 1936 to 1960. Briggs also assisted the Garden Club of South Carolina with several projects, including the design of the South Carolina Memorial Garden in Columbia, honoring soldiers who served in World War II. In addition Briggs frequently advised on camellia shows and spring garden tours as well as giving lectures and conducting classes in landscape design. Briggs was made an honorary member of the Garden Club of Charleston in 1950 in recognition of his many contributions to the community and the state. The following examples describe selected civic and community projects in which Briggs played an important role.

The Gateway Walk

Following a trip to Paris in the late 1920s, which included an inspiring visit to La Madeleine Church and the surrounding gardens, Mrs. Clelia Peronneau McGowan returned home with a desire to create a similar setting in the heart of her native Charleston. Employing her persuasive skills as president of the Garden Club of Charleston and as an influential member of the Charleston City Council, Mrs. McGowan was successful in bringing her dream to reality with the development of Charleston's Gateway Walk.

Dedicated on April 10, 1930, to coincide with the 250th anniversary of the founding of the city, Gateway Walk combined several historic sites with an interconnecting system of landscaped walkways in Charleston's historic district. Beginning on Archdale Street in St. John's Lutheran and Unitarian churchyards, Gateway Walk continued across King Street through the grounds of the Charleston Library Society. From here the walk crossed Meeting Street, passed the Congregational Church, and concluded at St. Philip's Episcopal Church. The name "Gateway Walk" was derived from the fact that visitors passed through ten wrought-iron gates as they traveled the length of the walk.

Based on a plan prepared by Briggs, Gateway Walk was designed to provide visitors a series of experiences that appealed to the senses—historic monuments, beautiful wrought-iron gates, ornate

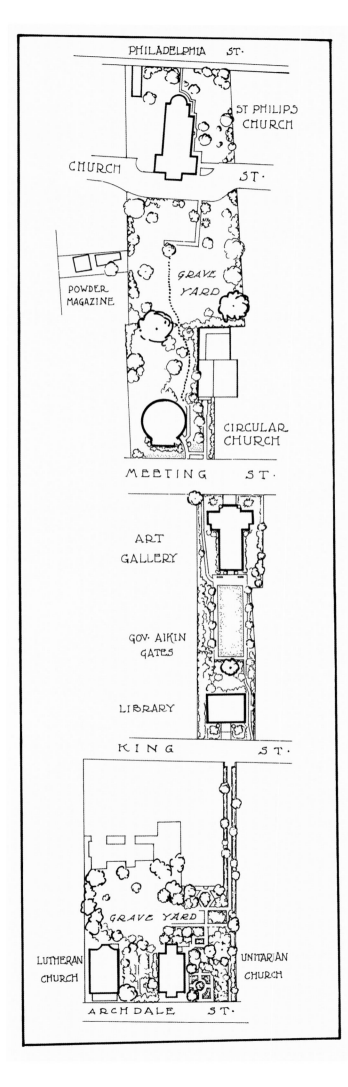

GATEWAY WALK

A WALKING TOUR THROUGH THE HEART OF THE HISTORIC DISTRICT

Gateway, St. John's Church

A PROJECT OF THE GARDEN CLUB OF CHARLESTON

Plan and brochure for Gateway Walk, designed by Briggs to carry visitors through four of Charleston's oldest churchyards, past ornate monuments, wrought-iron gates, decorative fences, flowering plants, and ancient live-oak trees

Beginning on Archdale Street in the St. John's Lutheran and Unitarian churchyards, Gateway Walk ends at the historic cemetery and churchyard of St. Philip's Episcopal Church.

fences, and a variety of ornamental plants, including azaleas, camellias, dogwood, flowering bulbs, and live-oak trees. Gateway Walk was an instant success, bringing pleasure to visitors and local citizens alike.

During World War II it became increasingly difficult to secure funds and resources to maintain Gateway Walk, and by 1950 the project had begun to show signs of neglect. In January 1953 the Garden Club of Charleston took steps to restore the walk to its former glory. A special restoration committee, chaired by Mrs. Henry P. Staats, was appointed to work with Briggs to minimize maintenance of Gateway Walk while retaining the historic integrity of its original design. Restoration was finalized by the end of the year, and a dedication ceremony was held on December 8, 1953. In recognition of its importance to the community, the project was awarded the Kellogg Medal for Civic Achievement in 1954.

The Garden Club of Charleston approved a second restoration of Gateway Walk in 1992—some fifteen years after Briggs' death. This effort was carried out in association with local landscape architect T. Hunter McEaddy. The restoration was planned to coincide with the seventieth anniversary of the Garden Club of Charleston. In concert with a formal dedication of this second restoration effort, a memorial tree planting was held to honor Loutrel Briggs' efforts and contributions to Gateway Walk and to recognize his "time and talent to help beautify Charleston." The following poem by Clelia McGowan, offers a poignant description of a community project that has brought pleasure to visitors and local residents alike:

> Through hand-wrought gates, alluring paths
>   Lead on to pleasant places,
> Where ghosts of long-forgotten things
>   Have left elusive traces.

The Heyward-Washington House Garden

Located at 87 Church Street, adjacent to Catfish Row, the Heyward-Washington House was built circa 1770 by Daniel Heyward, a wealthy rice planter from St. Luke's Parish. The house was inherited by Daniel's son, Thomas Heyward, Jr., who served as a delegate to the Continental Congress and later became a signer of the Declaration of Independence. In May 1791 President George Washington stayed at the Heyward House while visiting the city, recording in his diary that the "lodgings provided for me in this place was very good, being the furnished house of a gentleman at present in the country." Since that time

THE GATEWAY WALK
OF THE GARDEN CLUB OF CHARLESTON.
THE WALK WAS OPENED APRIL 10TH, 1930,
THE 250TH ANNIVERSARY OF THE FOUNDING
OF CHARLES TOWN

THIS CENTRAL AREA WAS CREATED BY
THE GARDEN CLUB, WITH THE CO-OPERATION
OF THE MAYOR, THOMAS P. STONEY

LOUTREL W. BRIGGS   MRS. CLELIA P. McGOWAN
LANDSCAPE ARCHITECT   PRESIDENT OF THE GARDEN CLUB

COMMITTEE CHAIRMEN
MRS. BEVERLY MIKELL   MRS. W. S. LANNEAU   MRS. JOHN C. SIMONDS
MRS. W. B. RAVENEL, JR.   MRS. R. McIVER WILBUR

Plaque commemorating Gateway Walk

The 1953 restoration of Gateway Walk included additional plantings of flowers, shrubs, and trees in an effort to provide visual interest throughout the year.

The Heyward-Washington House garden is a re-creation
of a late-eighteenth-century Charleston garden.

the house has been known as the Heyward-
Washington House.

Following the destructive effects of the Civil War, the Heyward-Washington House went
through a period of decline until it was rescued
in the 1920s by a group of preservationists. The
house was purchased by the Charleston Museum
in 1929 and became Charleston's first house museum. In 1930 Emma Richardson, assistant director of the Charleston Museum, was given the task
of creating a period garden at the rear of the
property that would exemplify a late-eighteenth-
century Charleston garden.

After consulting many old garden plats, she
developed a geometric plan consisting of a long
rectangle that incorporated a circular motif with

concentric paths and brick-bordered beds. The
design was reviewed and approved by Albert Simons, architect in charge of the restoration of
the Heyward-Washington House, and Lt. Col.
Alston Deas, president of the Society for the Preservation of Old Dwellings.

Following the plan's approval, Ms. Richardson and a young assistant laid out the garden
using a yardstick and a piece of string. Many
friends generously gave old-fashioned plants from
their own gardens, while others made small gifts
of money to purchase additional plants and materials. As Washington had resided in the Heyward
House in 1791, it was decided to use only plants
that had been grown prior to that date. To accomplish this objective, Richardson developed a

The use of historic plants in the Heyward-Washington House garden creates an air of antiquity and Old World charm.

comprehensive list of historic plants using J. C. Loudon's *Encyclopedia of Plants,* a popular English garden book first published in 1828. Richardson's plant list was published in *The Heyward Washington Garden* (Charleston Museum leaflet no. 15), published in February 1941. The list includes many old garden favorites such as Stokes' aster, calendula, candytuft, English daisy, four-o'clock, hollyhock, lantana, marigold, nasturtium, snapdragon, stock, and violets. The Garden Club of Charleston assumed the responsibility for the care and maintenance of the garden in 1941 and has provided continuous support since that time.

Refinements to the Heyward-Washington House garden took place circa 1962, when the Garden Club of Charleston appointed Mrs. Frederick Richards, chairman of a restoration committee, to work with Loutrel Briggs on improvements to the garden. (Briggs had designed Mrs. Richards's garden at 100 Tradd Street in the 1930s and the two had become close personal friends.) Briggs provided professional services that included refinement of the garden's original design, the use of specific heirloom plants, and the selection and placement of appropriate garden furniture to enhance the historic character of the garden.

The South Carolina Memorial Garden

At its annual meeting in November 1944, the Garden Club of South Carolina voted to create a

The South Carolina Memorial Garden, which Briggs designed as a gift
to the Garden Club of South Carolina

memorial garden honoring those who served in World War II. Under the leadership of Mrs. Louis I. Guion, seventh president of the club, efforts were initiated to locate an appropriate site. Soon after the search began, Mrs. Samuel Boylston of Columbia offered the lower portion of her garden as a potential location. Located at 1919 Lincoln Street, on the corner of Calhoun and Lincoln streets in the city's historic Arsenal Hill district and one block from the Governor's Mansion, the site (approximately 220 feet long and 50 feet wide) proved ideal in terms of size and location.

The Garden Club of South Carolina accepted Mrs. Boylston's gracious offer and immediately began to plan for the development of the garden.

The next step in the process was the creation of an appropriate design that the Garden Club of South Carolina could implement as financial resources became available. No doubt because of his previous involvement in other garden club projects, Loutrel Briggs was contacted to prepare a design for the garden, which he agreed to create free of charge as a gift to the Garden Club of South Carolina and out of respect to those who served in World War II. Because of his skill and experience in creating gardens in areas of limited space, Briggs proved an ideal choice to design the Memorial Garden. His plan for the garden incorporated garden features such as a decorative wrought-iron entrance gate, garden sculpture, a

The South Carolina Memorial Garden was planted with a variety of traditional ornamentals including azaleas (above, left), yellow jessamine (above, right), and sasanquas (below).

fountain terrace, flagstone walks, selected garden furniture, a small gatehouse, a service building, and a variety of ornamental plants.

While work on the design of the Memorial Garden began in 1946, changes to the plan occurred as late as 1950 during trips Briggs made to Columbia to collaborate with the University of South Carolina Press on his forthcoming book, *Charleston Gardens.* During these visits Briggs offered suggestions on the selection and placement of a variety of plants, including boxwoods, star magnolias, camellias, azaleas, dogwoods, sasanquas, hollies, tea olives, crape myrtles, loquats, ivy, Carolina cherry laurel, and yellow jessamine (the state flower of South Carolina). Today the only surviving plan of the Memorial Garden is located in the archives of the South Carolina Historical Society in Charleston, South Carolina.

Because of limited funds the South Carolina Memorial Garden was not completed until the spring of 1957, at which time it was officially

Visitors to the South Carolina Memorial Garden in 1952: Mrs. Charles H. Haralson;
Mrs. C. D. F. O'Hern; Mrs. G. C. Spillers, national president of the State Garden Clubs;
Mrs. W. Bedford Moore, Jr.; and Mrs. Luther Burris

dedicated by Mrs. John Thomas (Cuba) Rutledge, president of the Garden Club of South
Carolina. Even though it took more than twelve
years before the project was fully implemented,
the Memorial Garden was recognized in 1946 for
its special contribution to South Carolina and the
region, as evidenced by an Achievement Award
for Exceptional Merit, given to the Garden Club
of South Carolina at the annual convention of the

National Council of State Garden Clubs held in
New Orleans. Not only was the project the nation's first memorial garden honoring those who
served in World War II, but it also served as an
inspiration for other civic-minded organizations
throughout the country. Today the South Carolina Memorial Garden remains a lasting legacy to
the visionary efforts of the Garden Club of South
Carolina and the contributions of Loutrel Briggs.

Chapter Six

❧

Briggs' Gardens

BRIGGS' PHILOSOPHY regarding garden design was influenced by his training as a landscape architect and his travels abroad to visit and study the great gardens of Europe. In an interview with Rowena Wilson Tobias published in the *News and Courier* on February 23, 1941, Briggs offered the following comments on garden design: "Here in America we have developed the profession of landscape architecture, a combination of both architecture and horticulture, more than in any other country. Gardens used to be designed by architects, by artists, or occasionally by gardeners. But the best efforts can be attained by someone who combined all these qualities. The average American garden now is less architectural that the Italian, not so stiffly patterned as the French, nor so abundantly planted as the English. We are developing a distinct type, following the English precedent more than any other, which is a happy combination of architectural quality and planting design."

Following this trend, Briggs developed his own distinct style that embodied the idea of creating gardens that respected and complemented an individual space. Briggs also believed that, if at all possible, a garden should function as an outdoor room and be visible and easily accessible from the house in order to establish a close interior-exterior relationship between the house and garden. Briggs also placed great importance on understanding the needs of his clients. His ultimate desire was to create gardens that would bring continued pleasure to their owners and to develop creative and workable solutions that would satisfy their individual aesthetic and functional needs.

Briggs designed more than one hundred gardens in Charleston and the Carolina lowcountry, each fashioned to respect the unique conditions and character of the site. The layout of each garden was never repeated from a previous design. Briggs' creative skills as a garden designer were unparalleled at the time. His innovative and imaginative designs for Charleston's city and plantation gardens are a lasting testimony to Briggs' skills as a talented garden designer.

The following Charleston gardens have been selected as representative examples of Loutrel Briggs' marvelous talent as a garden designer. Each design addressed challenges resulting from a variety of historic, cultural, spatial, and environmental conditions, and in every case Briggs successfully developed a creative solution that has withstood the test of time.

The William Gibbes House and Garden

Located at 64 South Battery, the William Gibbes House was built circa 1772 by William Gibbes, one of Charleston's wealthiest colonial merchant-planters. During the Revolutionary War, Gibbes was evicted from the property by the British and imprisoned in St. Augustine, Florida. He returned to Charleston at the end of the war and occupied the house until his death in 1789. A subsequent owner of the property was the Reverend John Grimké-Drayton, who developed Magnolia

Gardens—noted for its informal plantings or camellias and azaleas.

In 1928, the William Gibbes House was purchased by Mrs. Washington (Cornelia) Roebling, a native South Carolinian. Cornelia had lived in Charleston during her first marriage, to John B. Farrow, who died in 1893. In 1903 she married Washington Augustus Roebling of Trenton, New Jersey. After his death in 1926, Mrs. Roebling returned to Charleston and purchased the historic William Gibbes House in 1928.

For the restoration of the grounds, she engaged the services of Loutrel Briggs. As Briggs had not yet opened a Charleston office, it is assumed that Mrs. Roebling knew of his work in the North and offered him his first commission in Charleston. Mrs. Roebling insisted that the new garden for the William Gibbes House be designed in the spirit of the past. Briggs' design was based on remnants of an earlier, eighteenth-century parterre garden that had existed on the grounds.

Other features included an enclosed flagstone terrace at the rear of the house and a long axial walk that extended from the terrace to a historic summerhouse dating from the Grimké-Drayton period, located at the back of the property. In the northeast corner of the property, Briggs designed a large formal garden with a central pool and fountain, box-bordered beds, ornamental shrubs, trees, and seasonal plantings. The watercolor rendering of the formal garden by J. Floyd Yewell, featured in the January 1932 issue of *Country Life,* captured the spirit of the garden by depicting architectural features and plantings in soft pastel colors to create an image of a Charleston garden in spring.

The Roebling garden was also featured in the 1931 *Year Book of the Architectural League of New York,* the January 15, 1933, issue of *Town and Country* magazine, the March 1933 issue of *House and Garden,* and the June 1936 issue of the *American Architect and Architecture.* Inclusion of Briggs' work in a variety of respected publications and

The William Gibbes House

Left: J. Floyd Yewell's romanticized rendering of the Washington Roebling garden in spring

magazines provided him with national exposure. No doubt this publicity led to numerous commissions from wealthy northerners, who at the time were purchasing Charleston townhouses and plantations in the Carolina lowcountry as winter retreats or hunting preserves.

Mulberry Plantation

Mulberry Plantation, often referred to as Mulberry Castle, is located on the western branch of the Cooper River in Berkeley County, approximately thirty miles north of Charleston. Built circa 1714 by Englishman Thomas Broughton—

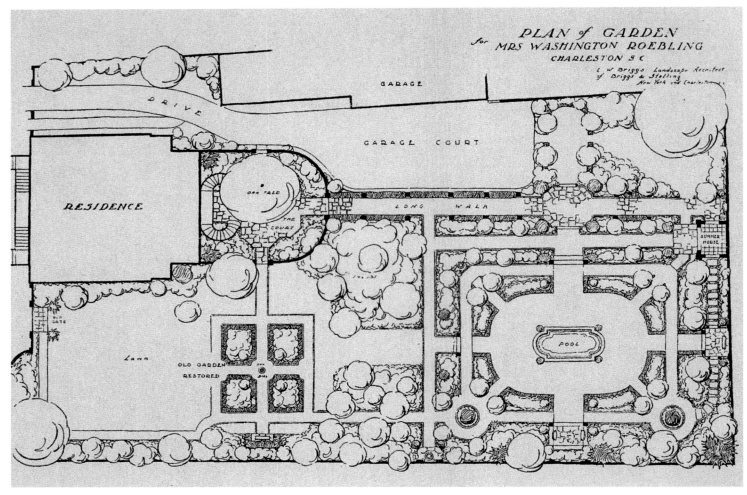

A plan of the Washington Roebling garden

a planter and later royal governor of South Carolina—Mulberry derived its name from the Mulberry trees grown on the plantation during the colonial period for the production of silk. Following silk and later indigo, rice became the major cash crop at Mulberry and was grown there until around 1902.

At the end of the Civil War, Mulberry passed through the hands of several owners until it was purchased in 1915 by Clarence W. Chapman, a New York financier whose principal interests were mining and shipbuilding. Chapman was one of the first northerners to purchase a lowcountry plantation as a winter retreat—a practice that accelerated in the 1920s and 1930s.

After purchasing Mulberry, Mr. and Mrs. Chapman commissioned the English architect Charles Brendon to prepare plans for the restoration of the house and selected Briggs to design the grounds. As no remains of an earlier garden existed on the property, the historic character of the house and the natural beauty of the site served as inspiration for Briggs' design. Mulberry's elevated position on a commanding bluff overlooking the Cooper River and old rice fields—along with ancient live-oak trees, old cedars, and lofty pines—provided Briggs with a perfect setting for a design that capitalized on the natural views and vistas of the surrounding landscape. Briggs took advantage of Mulberry's elevation to create a series of connecting gardens on three separate levels.

The design Briggs developed for Mulberry in 1930 included a new entrance court (which he

Mulberry Plantation

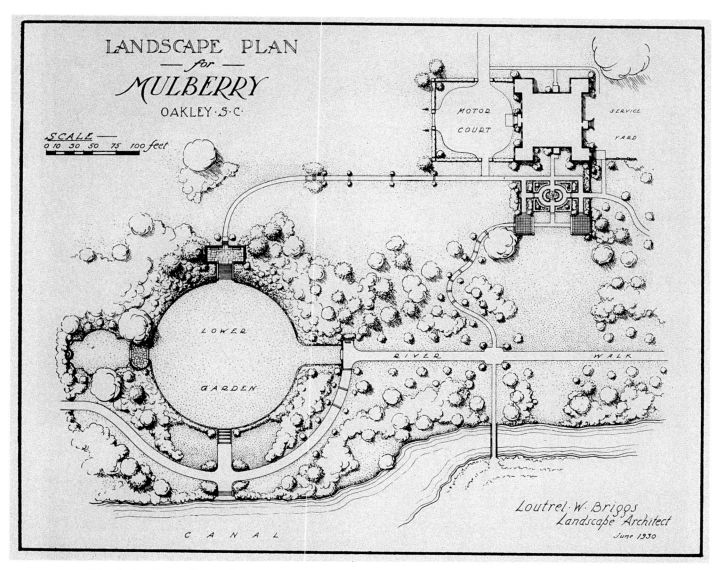

LANDSCAPE PLAN
— for —
MULBERRY
OAKLEY · S · C ·

SCALE
0 10 30 50 75 100 feet

MOTOR COURT

SERVICE YARD

LOWER

GARDEN

RIVER   WALK

CANAL

Loutrel · W · Briggs
Landscape Architect
June 1930

Briggs' plan for Mulberry Plantation

The east side of the house, where Briggs designed a boxwood
parterre and two brick terraces overlooking historic rice fields

referred to as a motor court) in front of the house. The arrival court was defined by selectively placed square brick piers connected by a clipped pittosporum hedge with the outer corners being planted with native cedars (*Juniperius virginiana*). This formal arrangement provided a perfect setting for the western facade of the house—creating a prominent sense of place and a "stage" from which the surrounding landscape could be viewed and admired. To the east of the house, Briggs designed a boxwood parterre with two brick terraces on either end. Overlooking spectacular views of historic rice fields, the terraces were enclosed with open-grill ironwork in decorative designs—allowing for an unrestricted view of the Cooper River and an old canal that had been used in the past to carry fresh water to the rice fields.

Several paths extended from the east side of the house down a gentle slope to an informal camellia garden. From the entrance court, a walk led to a lower terrace with steps leading down to a garden below. The lower garden, the centerpiece of which was a large circular lawn, was surrounded by azaleas, camellias, and flowering shrubs. Many of the plants were purchased from Carolina Floral Nursery—established in 1911 and located a short distance away in Mount Holly. On seeing Mulberry, E. T. H. Shaffer, author of *Carolina Gardens* (1937), wrote: "For romantic story, beauty of location, sympathy and perfection in execution, I have found no finer garden anywhere than at Mulberry-on-Cooper."

In 1930 Briggs also designed a garden for the Chapmans' summer home in the Ramapo River valley in northern New Jersey. Mr. Chapman named this estate "Welawiben," a word created to connote good heath and fellowship. Located on several hundred acres outside Mahwah, New Jersey, the main house, designed in the casual style of Hudson River valley homes, provided a commanding view of the surrounding countryside. The property was purchased by the Catholic Church in 1954 and developed as a religious retreat, now known as the Carmel Retreat Center.

Mepkin Plantation

Mepkin Plantation is located on the west branch of the Cooper River, some thirty miles upstream from Charleston. In 1762 Henry Laurens, an early American patriot born in Charleston in 1724, purchased Mepkin from John Colleton of Middlesex, England. Laurens used the land to grow indigo and cotton as a means of supplementing his mercantile business in Charleston. After Henry Laurens died in 1792, Mepkin remained in the Laurens family until 1851. Thereafter the property passed through several hands, until it was purchased in 1916 by John Johnson, a wealthy New York businessman who used the property as a hunting preserve.

In 1936 New York publisher Henry R. Luce and his wife, Clare Boothe Luce, acquired Mepkin as a winter retreat. The Luces also maintained a summer home in Ridgefield, Connecticut. When he bought Mepkin, Henry Luce was the editor of *Time, Life, Fortune,* and *Sports Illustrated* magazines while Mrs. Luce was editor of *Vanity Fair.* In 1942 she was elected to Congress and in 1953 became U.S. ambassador to Italy. The Luces' interest in modern architecture led to their selection of the well-known architect Edward Durrell Stone to design a complex of buildings at Mepkin for living and entertaining during the winter months. Stone was one of the first American architects to embrace the International Style. An important example of his work is the John F. Kennedy Cultural Center in Washington, D.C. The residential compound Stone designed at Mepkin consisted of a main house, three one-story guest houses, and a series of outbuildings. "Architecture: Modern in South Carolina," an article published in the August 1937 issue of *House and Garden,* reported: "Edward D. Stone, noted New York architect designed a complex of buildings for the Luces and at this year's exhibition of the New York League his design was awarded the medal for domestic architecture.

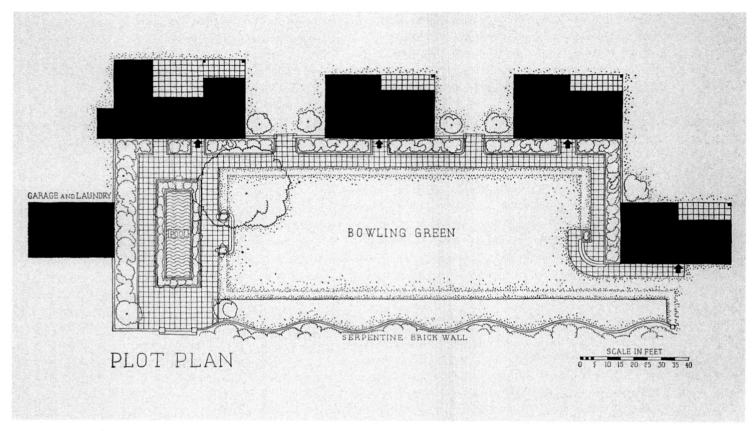

PLOT PLAN

GARAGE AND LAUNDRY

POOL

BOWLING GREEN

SERPENTINE BRICK WALL

SCALE IN FEET
0 5 10 15 20 25 30 35 40

The site plan Briggs prepared for Mepkin shows a creative layout including a primary residence
and three guesthouses located along a central open space or "bowling green."

Mr. Stone, in the most recent example of his work, has made a notable contribution to modern architecture by investing his design with those qualities of simple grace and dignity which are properly considered essential in residential architecture. . . ."

The Luces commissioned Briggs to design the garden and grounds at Mepkin. Briggs found Mrs. Luce an appreciative and personable client, commenting in a February 23, 1940, article in the *News and Courier:* "Mrs. Luce is a most charming client, keenly interested in gardens. . . . Her enthusiasm makes the work there [at Mepkin] very pleasant." In *Charleston Gardens* Briggs describes his design for Mepkin as follows:

The gardens around which the buildings are grouped conformed to the new style in order to provide a suitable setting for the architecture, but beyond its boundaries the landscape scheme was inspired by the ageless beauty with which nature endowed this lovely location. Walks wander through the woods, into which are woven azaleas and other spring flowering shrubs, two little lakes lie in a ravine and near them is a terraced garden which slopes toward the river, the last level is designed to frame the view over the water and marshes beyond. A live oak occupied the center of the site and was retained as a focal point for the crossing of the two axes of the plan. The longer one extends up from the shore in a series of grass parcels, separated by wide steps and terminated at a low retaining wall with steps on each side. . . . The shorter axes connects the walks along the lower lakes with high ground above the garden. In

One of the guesthouses at Mepkin

planning the more open areas, the graceful undulating contours of the land were emphasized by spacious uninterrupted stretches of lawn or limited low plantings, with camellias occasionally used for accent.

Briggs' design capitalized on the natural features and beauty of the property—live oaks, magnolias, undulating terrain, and dramatic views—to develop a marvelous design solution that respected the simple lines of Stone's modern architectural style, while preserving the inherent beauty of the site.

In 1944 Ann Brokaw, Mrs. Luce's daughter from a previous marriage, was killed in an automobile accident. In coping with this tragedy, Mrs. Luce converted to the Catholic faith, and in 1949 she donated Mepkin to the Catholic Diocese of Charleston for use as a Trappist monastery. Both

Henry and Clare Boothe Luce, along with her daughter and mother, are interred in a small cemetery located at the top of Mepkin's terraced garden, shaded by over-hanging branches of ancient live-oak trees.

Emily Whaley's Garden

One of the best known and most highly publicized of Loutrel Briggs' Charleston gardens was designed in 1940 for Emily and Ben Scott Whaley at 58 Church Street. Having seen several Charleston gardens designed by Briggs, including one designed for her friend Mrs. Frederick (Sara Ann) Richards at 100 Tradd Street, Emily Whaley convinced her husband that she too should have a garden designed by Briggs. She describes the process of working with Briggs in her book *Mrs. Whaley and Her Charleston Garden* (1997):

From the "bowling green" at Mepkin, walks wandered through shaded woodlands to a terraced garden entered through a decorative garden gate (right). The terraced garden was designed with a central axis that extended from an upper level to the Cooper River and marshes beyond (above).

Our Church Street plot wasn't large—only 30 by 110 feet—but it had several natural advantages. It lay at the east end of our house, which kept the hot afternoon sun from baking it. At the far end was the ancient high brick wall of a neighbor's carriage house. Plus, there were sizeable handsome trees in the lot to the left and right. . . . We explained [to Briggs] beforehand that the garden would be completed in sections—first because the children were young and they and their friends used three-fourths of the area for a play ground and second, because we had money enough only to get one section going. We would continue the project as the children outgrew the swings, sandbox, and basketball hoop and as we had additional funds.

Mr. Briggs asked what type of garden we liked, formal or casual? How much area we wanted for bulbs, annuals, and perennials? How much for azaleas and camellias? Did we want a patio? Did we want plants to bloom over the whole year or did we prefer to concentrate the bloom during certain months of the year? We finally chose a romantic natural background with a formal foreground. Green predominates during the summer and early fall, while the bloom is concentrated from October through May.

That was it. In half an hour he formulated a plan and put it on paper. . . . I liked what I saw and told him so. In ten days or so he brought us a blueprint and also a colored crayon sketch of what he thought the garden would

Wrought-iron gate at the entrance to Emily Whaley's garden. The gate opens onto a flagstone path that winds through a variety of shade-loving plants, including camellias, azaleas, loquats, podocarpus, holly ferns, Japanese box, and fatsia. Views along the path create a feeling of anticipation and discovery of the garden that beckons beyond.

Right: Emily Whaley's garden in spring

look like in ten years time. From then on we were on our own. . . .

The design of the garden was laid out along a central axis that extended from a small terrace adjacent to the house to the rear of the property. The plan was based on a concept that included three distinct garden rooms. The first was elliptical in shape—the central portion of which was planted in grass and flanked by planting beds filled with colorful annuals, perennials, and flowering shrubs. A brick border was used to articulate the design and to separate the lawn from the adjourning planting beds.

Typical plantings within the flower borders included tulips, iris, jonquils, stock, snapdragons, and pansies in the spring, followed by salvia, alyssum, begonias, geraniums, impatiens, verbena, phlox, lantana, dahlias, nicotiana, and plumbago in summer. Roses, star jasmine, and other flowering vines were planted on fences that separated the garden from neighboring properties.

The next garden room was circular in design. The central portion was planted with grass while the surrounding borders were filled with Japanese box, pittosporum, azaleas, and camellias. The grass and planting beds were separated by an edging of old brick to define the design and add a feeling of age. A small circular pool, only 1½ inches deep, was located in the center of the lawn and served as a major focal point as well as a magnet for birds. The pool's mirrorlike surface reflected the colors of surrounding plants and flowers.

The second and third garden rooms were partially separated by low pierced-brick walls placed perpendicular to the main axis of the garden. These served as transition elements between the two formal, sunny areas of the garden and the remaining shaded garden room, which was informal in design. The third garden room was paved with brick in an oval form and was surrounded by plantings of azaleas, camellias, and hydrangeas as well as ferns and other shade-loving plants. A spreading oak from an adjourning property provided a canopy of green at the rear garden adding a sense of tranquility and repose.

The garden contained a number of decorative features. A white scalloped-wood fence offered privacy; small garden sculptures added interest and accent; garden benches provided the opportunity for relaxation and enjoyment; and decorative urns, pots, and containers planted with annuals added seasonal color and charm.

An assortment of garden furnishings and accessories were carefully selected and placed in Emily Whaley's garden to add visual interest and complement the overall design.

Right: The Willcox garden at 2 King Street. Photograph by Alexander Wallace

This elegant town garden combined Briggs' imaginative design and creative plant compositions fashioned by Emily Whaley. While the basic design of the garden has remained constant over time, plantings have changed as Mrs. Whaley experimented with various arrangements and color combinations. The garden was featured in such notable books as Rosemary Verey and Ellen Samuels' *The American Woman's Garden* (1984), Caroline Boisset's *Town Gardens* (1989), and Emily Whaley's own *Mrs. Whaley and Her Charleston Garden.* Over time Mrs. Whaley's garden gained international recognition as one of Charleston's finest town gardens. Noted English garden writer Rosemary Verey is quoted in the spring 1987 issue of *Hortus* as saying: "This could be my dream garden, with its thoughtful planting, a pool for reflections, a seat among the scented flowers, and shadows. Whichever way you look, up or down the garden, you feel the essential qualities of continuity and peace."

The Willcox Garden

Located at 2 King Street just around the corner from White Point Garden, this small gem of a garden was designed by Loutrel Briggs for Mr. and Mrs. Lloyd Willcox in 1951. Protected behind high brick walls, the garden was entered through a decorative wrought-iron gate that was almost always left open in spring when the garden was in full bloom.

Once inside the garden, the visitor was drawn to a long shaded path extending along the side of the house to a rear entrance featuring an arched stucco wall, which served as an interesting focal point and backdrop for garden ornaments and pots of seasonal plants. To the left of the garden gate, a flagstone walk led to the main entrance of

The Willcox garden in spring. Walls were softened with plantings, and several garden features were strategically placed to add interest and variety to the overall scene.

the house past a series of perfectly proportional outdoor rooms. Each room was defined by a low brick wall or a clipped hedge of Japanese box. Slight changes of elevation in the garden created a feeling of spaciousness and added interest to the overall design.

A small covered porch located along the front of the house offered an ideal spot from which the garden could be seen and enjoyed. The porch was attractively furnished with colorful pots of geraniums in spring and hanging baskets of begonias and impatiens in summer. A small seating area located under the spreading canopy of

a large hackberry tree in the northeast corner of the garden served as a perfect location to catch the warm morning sun and to gain a different perspective of the garden as it changed with the light during the course of the day.

The stucco walls surrounding the garden were covered with ivy and softened with plantings of azaleas, camellias, aucuba, and nandinas. Lush plantings of cleyera, fatshedera, podocarpus, and holly fern were used to add seasonal interest and provide a finished look to the garden. In spring the garden was filled with flowering bulbs and annuals to create a striking display

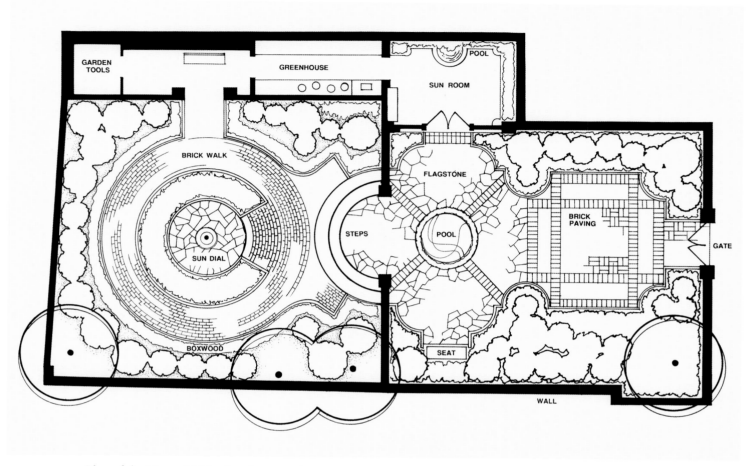

Plan of the Hagoods' Meeting Street garden

of seasonal color. Several decorative features, including a small wall fountain, added visual interest and personal charm to the garden. The Willcox garden, like many other Charleston gardens that are enclosed by high walls, was endowed with a protected microclimate in which a variety of exotic and tender plants could be grown twelve months of the year.

The Hagood Garden

Located at 23 Meeting Street in the heart of Charleston's historic district, this small city garden was designed by Loutrel Briggs for Mr. and Mrs. James Hagood in 1969. This was the second garden Briggs designed for the Hagoods—the first being a much larger garden at 16 Legare

Street in 1947. Briggs was often engaged by previous clients to design a second garden when a new house was purchased or when revisions to an existing garden were desired.

The area in which the garden was built at 23 Meeting Street was a small rectangular space no larger than forty-five feet wide and fifty feet long. The garden was divided into two outdoor rooms separated by a slight change of grade to add interest and visual appeal. The first room consisted of a small paved terrace enclosed by a pierced-brick wall and softened by mixed plantings of ornamental shrubs. A small circular pool served as a focal point of the garden. Along the outer rim of the pool was a small planting area filled with flowering plants to provide color and seasonal

View from the entrance gate of the Hagood garden at 23 Meeting Street. The eye is drawn
into the garden by a series of focal points that articulate and enhance the overall design.
Briggs had earlier designed a garden for the Hagoods at 16 Legare Street.

Left: The Hagood garden, a delightful walled garden blending natural and hardscape elements.
The generous use of brick and bluestone paving helped define individual garden rooms and
reduce ongoing maintenance.

interest. A small sunroom adjoining the house
contained exotic plants, a small wall fountain,
and decorative garden furniture. The sunroom
provided a visual connection to the garden
throughout the year.

The second garden room was paved with
brick in a circular pattern. An antique sundial
served as the central feature of the design. This
area of the garden was planted with a variety of
evergreen shrubs, several small trees, and flowering plants. A low, clipped hedge of Japanese box
was used to articulate the design. Old brick, flagstone paving, mature plants, and historic garden
features made the garden look and feel much
older than it actually was. A small storage area for
tools was incorporated at the rear of the house.

In *Gardens of the American South* (1971), John
Wedda commented on the special character and
design of the Hagood garden: "Not everyone can
view a block of granite or a piece of wood and

see within its exterior surface and dimensions
all that is necessary for the creation of new beauty. The magic is the alchemy of art which can
transform raw materials into thoroughly realized
form, texture, and color. The gardener is artist,
tool, and medium working in collaboration with
the ultimate artist, nature. In this garden there
were two artists in collaboration: Mrs. Hagood,
a former garden club president, and Mr. Loutrel
Briggs, a noted landscape architect and horticulturist."

The Mills House Hotel Courtyard

One of Loutrel Briggs' most public, yet least
known, projects is the courtyard garden of the
Mills House Hotel at 115 Meeting Street in
Charleston. The original hotel was constructed
in 1853 by Otis Mills, a native of Massachusetts.
Described shortly after its completion as "the
finest hotel south of New York," the Mills House

Briggs' decorative layout in the courtyard paving at the Mills House Hotel simulates a formal eighteenth-century French parterre design.

Left: The courtyard garden of the Mills House Hotel, one of Briggs' most creative public designs. The antique fountain serves as the centerpiece.

served as the central feature of the design. This area of the garden was planted with a variety of evergreen shrubs, several small trees, and flowering plants. A low, clipped hedge of Japanese box was used to articulate the design. Old brick, flagstone paving, mature plants, and historic garden features made the garden look and feel much older than it actually was. A small storage area for tools was incorporated at the rear of the house.

In *Gardens of the American South* (1971), John Wedda commented on the special character and design of the Hagood garden: "Not everyone can view a block of granite or a piece of wood and see within its exterior surface and dimensions all that is necessary for the creation of new beauty. The magic is the alchemy of art which can transform raw materials into thoroughly realized form, texture, and color. The gardener is artist, tool, and medium working in collaboration with the ultimate artist, nature. In this garden there were two artists in collaboration: Mrs. Hagood, a former garden club president, and Mr. Loutrel

The Mills House courtyard garden

decorative wrought-iron fountain served as the central focal point of the courtyard. The plan of the courtyard garden is believed to have been inspired by a design in an eighteenth-century French pattern book of period garden designs.

Not only could the design of the courtyard be enjoyed at ground level, it was also visible from an elevated terrace and the upper-level rooms of the hotel. In each corner of the courtyard, Briggs incorporated four planting beds that were planted with camellias, azaleas, and evergreens to provide seasonal color and visual appeal. A decorative stucco wall and wooden-lattice gate with brick piers was located along the south wall of the courtyard to provide service access and to create the feeling of an intimate Charleston garden.

The Mills House courtyard remains a pleasant space for outdoor dining and social events in downtown Charleston.

A Lasting Legacy

The gardens previously described represent only a small number of the many projects Briggs designed during his nearly sixty-year career as a landscape architect. His enormous body of work is a lasting testament to his versatile talents and skills as one of the most important and influential designers in Charleston and the Carolina low-country during the first half of the twentieth century. His legacy remains today in the many gardens, both large and small, that are treasured for their enduring beauty and charm.

Chapter Seven

❧

Briggs' Design Style

WHILE BRIGGS' PROJECTS ran the gamut from college campuses, church grounds, and parks to housing projects and suburban estates, from all accounts he appears to have gained the greatest satisfaction and enjoyment from the design of small gardens. In designing Charleston's small gardens, Briggs adhered to several principles that proved of tremendous benefit throughout his career. He believed that each space and its surroundings should be carefully considered in determining the design of the garden. He also believed that, if at all possible, a close relationship should be developed between the house and garden plan. Briggs' desire was to create a garden that served as an outdoor room.

Briggs also placed great importance on understanding the desires of his clients. His ultimate objective was to create gardens that would bring continuous pleasure to their owners and satisfy their individual needs. Briggs is quoted in the April 15, 1973, edition of the *News and Courier* as saying that, when he undertook a landscape project, "two people had to be satisfied with the results, the client and me. My principle in working is not to make my friends my clients, but to make my clients my friends." Briggs was obviously successful in this endeavor as many of his clients became lifelong friends and frequently commissioned him to update an original design or create a new garden at a different location.

In the April 15, 1973, article, Briggs noted: "There is more to designing a garden than meets the eye. A great deal depends on the arrangement of adjoining architecture. . . . You can't take a preconceived design and put it on the ground. It won't work. You have to deal with a particular space and surroundings. . . . " Briggs believed that the most important requirement of a successful garden was "pictorial quality." He felt that, contrary to popular opinion, landscape design is one of the most difficult of all the arts because it requires the artistic imagination of a landscape painter and the skill of a sculptor to compose in three dimensions. Furthermore it requires engineering acumen to design walks, steps, terraces, and pools and the knowledge of a horticulturist in the proper selection and composition of ornamental plants. Over time Briggs developed a distinctive approach to the design of Charleston's small gardens that was appropriate to the climate, architecture, historic setting, and lifestyle of the city.

Briggs generally prepared his landscape plans and drawings using either pencil or ink on tracing paper. When a project was simple, he normally incorporated his design concept, plant selections, and construction details on a single sheet. In instances where a project was complex, Briggs prepared several drawings to provide a greater level of detail for ease of implementation. He frequently included sketches of walls, trellises, pools, and focal points on his drawings. These were shown as sections or simple perspectives to convey design concepts. Briggs' skill at supplementing his designs with sketches no doubt reflected his early training in art at the Art Students League of New York.

An East Bay garden designed by Briggs

Briggs' marvelous talent for garden design is evident in the many small and delightful gardens he designed in Charleston throughout his career. Designing these small gardens presented many challenges and obstacles because of their odd and erratic shapes, as well as shade, access, and spatial limitations. Briggs possessed an unusual talent to work within the constraints of limited space to fashion creative and imaginative designs. In "The Walled Gardens of Charleston," an article in *Horticulture* magazine (April 1988), Rosemary Verey described the challenges facing a designer in creating a successful garden in the city's small urban spaces:

Many of the homes and public buildings of Charleston date from the mid-1750s, when this colony was under English jurisdiction. Behind the fine door ways, white porticoes and balconies with slender, elegant columns, and the distinctive wrought-iron gateways that front on the streets lie small gardens, carefully planned, inviting yet mysterious.

Creating a garden in such limited space is the challenge of making a beautiful picture, framed by high walls, overhanging trees, carriage houses, and other immovable structures. A designer may find it easy to fashion a landscape with long vistas and a variety of elements, but being confined by space demands a strength of discipline, the ability to see from all angles, to appreciate in all directions, to create a picture within the smallest and most unpropitious corner.

The designer has the luxury of using jewels, so small and precious that they would be overwhelmed and lost in a larger, more spacious setting. He must be conscious of a feeling of intimacy, remembering how the garden will be seen from the windows and by visitors as they

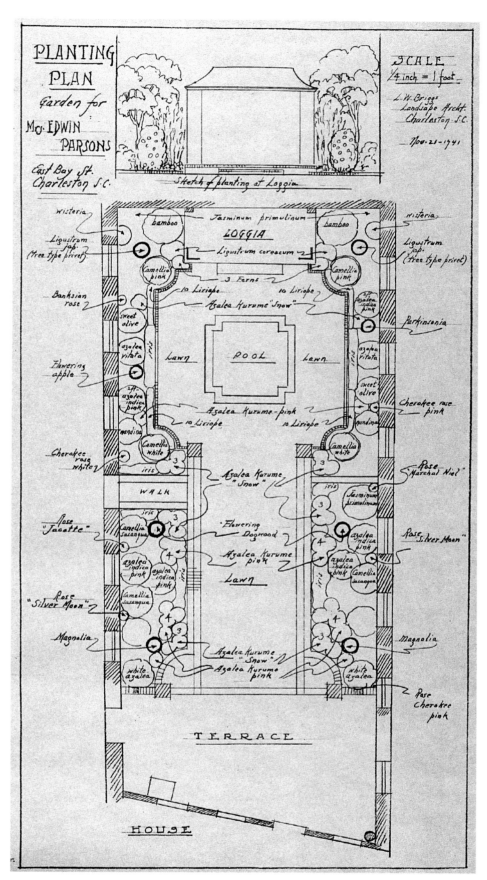

The layout plan of the East Bay garden reflects Briggs' design style
and presentation techniques.

A small Charleston garden inspired by Briggs' garden style. A variety of accessories and garden features help transform the garden into an outdoor room that could be enjoyed year round.

arrive. He must study the reflections, the shafts of light at each hour of the day and each season. There must be the essence of tranquility, no agitation or urge to move on. It should inspire in the beholder a sense of completion and satisfaction.

There should be a limitation of flowers, and by necessity there will be, because the choices will be dictated by the spaces and the microclimates created by the surrounding houses, the walls casting shade but reflecting warmth and keeping away the wind. Pierced walls help the air to circulate, and this is important in winter as well as in the summer, for as cold air sinks the frost will stay unless it is moved on, encouraged away by a breeze. Hot days need a special cool area with appropriate surroundings, so when evening brings relief from the high temperatures, there are the seat, the pool, and

the evening-scented plants awaiting you. In the same way, there should be framed views to enjoy from inside. . . . All must flow, yet be separated quietly into the suggestion of rooms.

Briggs was uniquely qualified to address each of the challenges facing a designer to create successful gardens in Charleston's small urban spaces. It was through his design skills that Charleston's city gardens reached their highest state of refinement. In designing more than one hundred small gardens in Charleston's historic district from the late 1920s through the 1970s, Briggs developed what is generally referred to today as "Charleston's Garden Style." He also played an important role in defining Charleston's image as a city of lovely walled gardens, secluded courtyards, and private garden sanctuaries. Today Briggs' gardens continue to inspire landscape architects, garden

A small Church Street garden. Briggs developed individual design solutions
that respected and capitalized on the unique aspects and potential of each site.

designers, and homeowners alike in the creation
of gardens of limited space.

Important characteristics of a Briggs garden
include:

Application of the basic principles of design to
create outdoor garden rooms

Use of appropriate materials for terraces, walks,
walls, and edging to complement existing
hardscape elements in the surrounding landscape and architectural setting

Incorporation of walls, fences, and evergreen
hedges, as a means of defining the garden
space

An appropriate use of water in the form of pools
and fountains to add life and visual interest

Use of a variety of techniques and design schemes
to make a small garden space appear larger
than its actual size

Selection and placement of appropriate garden
features—statuary, urns, and small structures
to add scale and enhance the visual character
of a garden

Selection and use of a limited variety of ornamental plants to establish unity and an appropriate sense of scale

Attention to construction details that define and
sustain a design and ensure visual continuity
throughout time

Each of the above elements are discussed in greater detail in the following text.

Design Principles

Briggs relied on the basic principles of good design such as proportion, repetition, unity, and
scale to create a sense of harmony within an allot-
ted space. Consideration was given to everything

Historic materials Briggs used for walks, terraces, patios, and drives included brick,
Portland stone, slate, Belgium block, cobblestone, and Bermuda limestone.

A Crab Orchard stone walk in a delightful Anson Street garden

from plants, structures, paved areas, and accessories. In each garden Briggs designed, he developed an individual and creative design solution that respected and capitalized on the special natural and physical elements of the site.

Briggs developed his designs by beginning at the house and working outward to create a visual link with the overall garden space. To enhance the feeling of spaciousness, large-textured plants were, as a rule, employed close to the house, while medium- and fine-textured plants were gradually transitioned away from the house to create an appropriate sense of scale. Briggs believed that each space and its surroundings should be carefully considered to create gardens that served as "outdoor rooms." He incorporated features such as terraces, pools, and intimate sitting areas to ensure that the garden was enjoyed year round.

Hardscape Materials

Briggs often employed historic materials in his gardens as a means of creating design continuity and establishing a feeling of age. He frequently used items such as oversized "Old English" bricks and antique stone in the construction of walls, walks, steps, terraces, patios, pools, and edgings. The appropriate use of these historic materials helped to articulate and enhance a design and connect the garden visually to its surroundings.

Hardscape materials also helped reduce and minimize maintenance. Briggs employed paving materials such as Portland stone, Welsh slate, and cobblestones. These historic materials were originally brought to Charleston as the ballast of sailing ships and over time became building materials in the city's gardens and landscapes. Bermuda limestone, a material imported into Charleston during colonial times, was frequently

An example of the decorative walls and gates Briggs designed for many Charleston gardens

used by Briggs for walks and terraces. During the 1960s Briggs often used Crab Orchard stone, a durable sandstone from middle Tennessee for walks and terraces.

Physical Enclosure

Briggs was highly successful in developing appropriate solutions to define boundaries, screen views, and create outdoor garden rooms in small urban spaces. He achieved this through the use of walls, fences, trellises, and gates. He seldom employed wood fences in his designs because they required constant maintenance and also because he wanted to adhere to Charleston's traditional use of brick and stucco walls.

A distinguishing feature of many Briggs gardens was the use of pierced-brick walls—a

decorative design of open brick work, historically associated with southern gardens. Not only were pierced-brick walls an aesthetic element in a garden, but they also improved air circulation. The patterns in these walls were often unusual in design. Briggs often recommended using old brick in the construction of walls to add a feeling of age to a garden.

Pools and Fountains

Of the many features that can be used in a garden, water offers one of the greatest opportunities to add life and interest to an outdoor space. Appropriately described as the living spirit of a garden, water has the ability to focus attention on itself as few other elements in a garden can. Water can create many moods, ranging from the quiet serenity of a tranquil pool to the animated movement of a splashing fountain. The sound and movement of water appeals to the senses and adds relief and coolness to a garden on a hot summer day. Any opportunity to use water in a garden should always be taken, for a garden always fails to meet its maximum potential when water is missing.

In many of his small gardens Briggs employed water in the form of a splashing fountain or a small pool. The use of a small pool in a garden of limited space is comparable to the use of a mirror in an indoor room. Pools have the ability to reflect the surrounding colors of flowers and trees and to add light, depth, and a sense of spaciousness to the smallest of garden rooms. Briggs always argued against the inclusion of a swimming pool in a Charleston garden because of its visual impact, especially in gardens of limited space.

Illusion of Space

To make a small garden appear larger than its actual size, Briggs applied a variety of techniques. He often incorporated subtle changes in grade through the use of raised terraces, steps, or slightly elevated planting beds to establish a sense of spaciousness and create a distinct garden room. Briggs also used low, pierced-brick walls placed

Briggs frequently used pierced-brick walls as decorative garden features

Above and overleaf: Two wall fountains in Charleston gardens

Example of an outdoor garden room

perpendicular to the main axis of the garden to subdivide a space, achieving the effect of several individual garden rooms. In addition to using walls to divide a space, he employed circles and ovals to establish visual separation of one area of the garden from another. These subtle techniques, while simple in nature, were highly effective in deceiving the eye and making a garden appear larger in scale than its actual size.

Briggs often placed features such as benches, statuary, or decorative gates at the ends of cross axes to create secondary focal points that attracted one's eye away from the length of a long, linear space. Other techniques Briggs used to make a garden appear larger included such clever devices as false perspective, trompe l'oeil, circles and curves, mirrors, and plants with small-textured foliage.

Garden Features

Briggs possessed a special talent for enhancing the character of his designs by selecting appropriate garden features, including sculpture, urns, decorative pots, benches, and gates. Each of these elements was selected based on size and appropriateness to the overall design. These features were placed at strategic points—such as a central point in the garden or at the end of an axis—to create visual interest and achieve a dramatic effect.

Briggs often placed low brick walls perpendicular to the main axis of a garden
to create the effect of separate garden rooms.

A cleverly placed mirror at the end of an East Bay garden, one of the design techniques
Briggs employed to make small gardens appear larger than their actual size

Briggs frequently used decorative benches and small lead figures to provide visual interest
and create an appropriate sense of scale.

Garden features also helped to establish an appropriate sense of scale. Briggs frequently employed lead statues, ornamental benches, or specimen plants to create a pleasant garden scene. He also used small pools and fountains to add life, movement, and interest to a garden. Garden features are particularly useful in small gardens as they help to establish a garden's overall image and mood. Because of limited space and the greater perception of detail in a small garden, special care and attention must be given to the selection, placement, and scale of garden

features to achieve the most effective and dramatic results. It was Briggs' creative use of garden features and his genius for details that endowed his gardens with special character and visual appeal.

Ornamental Plants

A particular trademark of a Briggs garden was the sensitive use of appropriate plants. Briggs selected plants based on their individual character and ability to perform within the limitations of available space. Briggs' selective use of different

Antique iron work like that at the John Rutledge House on Broad Street (above) was incorporated as a decorative feature in a garden Briggs designed for Mr. and Mrs. J. A. Hagood on Legare Street (below).

Lantana

Azalea

Cherokee rose

plant species not only helped to unify a garden's design but also provided a strong sense of visual continuity. Briggs' palette of selected plants included many that had been grown in Charleston gardens during earlier times.

In many instances Briggs also incorporated into his designs a beautiful stretch of lawn or a flower border planted with perennials, annuals, and bulbs. Both camellias and azaleas played an important role in Briggs' gardens, not only for their early- and midspring bloom, but also because of their ability to thrive in Charleston's favorable climate and long growing season. A combination of natural, physical, and environmental factors are responsible for creating the rich diversity of plants grown in Charleston gardens. A representative list of plants Briggs commonly employed in Charleston gardens is provided in the following chapter. Briggs selected each plant based on its size, texture, scale, flowers, fragrance, and sustainability. A limited palette of plants was a hallmark of a Briggs garden.

This Church Street garden exemplifies careful attention to detail to create a perfectly proportioned outdoor garden room.

Design Implementation

Clients often retained Briggs to coordinate and oversee the work of landscape contractors hired to implement his garden plans. This provided him the opportunity to ensure that his designs were carried out in a professional manner. Briggs was particular in his selection of landscape contractors to implement his designs. One of his favorites was Marshall W. "Billy" Hills. A graduate of Clemson University with a degree in ornamental horticulture, Hills worked with Briggs for more than twenty years. Two highly respected masons, Pinckney Ezekiel and Clarence Middleton, often assisted Hills in the construction of walls, walks, steps, brick columns, terraces, and pools specified in Briggs' plans. Over time a deep sense of professional respect and admiration developed between Briggs and Hills. In a December 23, 1993, letter to the editor in the *Charleston News and Courier,* Hills shared "fond memories" of his working relationship and respect for Briggs:

A couple of years after graduating from college in 1949, I began a garden maintenance service in downtown Charleston. This was one of the first services of its type offered in the area. Through contacts with my clients, I had the pleasure of meeting Mr. Briggs. At that time, he was still designing many gardens. After seeing him several times and discussing horticulture in depth, he asked me to bid on some of his work.

Our friendship progressed with caution on his part. After some time he decided that he was very pleased with my landscape installations. We became very good friends and he became my mentor. My phone would often ring around 7:30 A.M. "Hills, this is Briggs. Come by the office at 9 o'clock. I want to discuss a plan with you." This went on for many years and during that time, I installed essentially all of his designs.

Chapter Eight

Ornamental Plants for Charleston Gardens

PLANTS ARE ONE of the most important elements in Charleston gardens. They add color, provide fragrance, and create seasonal interest throughout the year. Several factors account for the wide range of plants employed in Charleston gardens. These include the region's semitropical climate and its long growing season, which lasts almost ten months of the year. As a general rule, the first freeze of the winter season occurs in December with the last frost coming in mid- to late February. Charleston's continuous blooming season was described by DuBose Heyward, noted Charleston novelist, poet, and playwright: "Charleston's magnificent springtime display continues into May and June with the blossoms of southern magnolias, confederate jasmine, and roses in vivid hues of rose, pink and red. Even as the days grow warm and the humidity rises, Charleston's floral season lingers throughout the summer with the brilliant displays of oleanders, crape myrtle, trumpet vine, althaea, and the exotic fragrance of ginger lilies that last well into the fall. Charleston's mild winters are soon followed in late January with a display of camellias, pansies, narcissus, and daffodils that serve as harbingers of another glorious spring."

In a February 23, 1941, article in the *News and Courier,* Briggs is quoted as saying that when he first came to Charleston he was drawn by its picturesque quality and mild climate. He also noted that, as a landscape architect, he was attracted by the luxurious plant material and its rapid growth in this section of the country: "Gardens here have an initial advantage in that you can accomplish more in a short time with a southern garden than any other in the country. The plants which flourish in Charleston are naturally attractive, and have the advantage of being evergreen."

In observing Charleston's extensive array of trees, shrubs, vines, and ground covers, Briggs soon developed a palette of plants that he felt appropriate for use in Charleston gardens. His selective use of ornamental plants became a trademark of a Briggs garden. Briggs believed that each plant should be chosen based on its individual character and ability to conform to the limitations of available space. As he said in an interview published in the April 15, 1973, *News and Courier,* "Plants should be chosen with considerable care because each one has a very individual character. The garden designer often has to go to various nurseries to get the right specimens. . . . He must also find out what his clients' preferences and requirements are. Do they want the garden in bloom all year or just in the spring?" Briggs advised against the use of fast growing plants and trees as they would soon become too large and alter the delicate balance of scale and proportion in a small garden.

Briggs' list of plants for use in Charleston gardens included American natives, Old World favorites, and exotics from China and Japan. Each was ideally suited to the city's long growing season, mild climate, and sheltered microclimates created by protective garden walls. Briggs traditionally relied on plants that offered colorful spring bloom yet provided visual interest throughout the year. He emphasized creating

A variety of plants from Europe, the West Indies, South America, and Asia have traditionally been grown in Charleston gardens, including hydrangea (above, left), coral vine (above, right), and morning glory (below).

maximum floral display from mid-February to early June.

While plants were an important feature in Briggs' gardens, they were but one of a variety of elements in the overall design. Of equal importance were the physical layout, hardscape materials, landscape details, and appropriate garden features such as walls, terraces, walks, and pools. Each in combination with ornamental plants resulted in a unique work of art. Briggs' ability to bring these various elements together in his designs endowed his gardens with an enduring quality that make them as appropriate today as when they were originally designed. The following list of plants employed by Briggs in his designs is based on a comprehensive review of Briggs' garden plans in the archives at the South Carolina Historical Society. Briggs' traditional plant list of forty or fifty plants was expanded in instances where a garden was designed for an avid horticulturist or a client passionately interested in plants.

Briggs frequently used plants that could tolerate shade and grow in areas of limited space,
such as azaleas (above, left), pittosporum (above, right), and camellias (below).

Ground Covers

Ground covers are generally described as low-growing, evergreen plants—such as vinca, ivy, and liriope—that are used as a substitute for grass. In a broader sense, ground covers also include selected vines, perennials, and herbaceous material planted in mass to create a transition from a lawn, terrace, walk, or patio to adjoining beds of shrubs and trees. In Charleston gardens Briggs relied on a number of ground covers to address a variety of practical and aesthetic needs. Ground covers were particularly useful in many of the city's small gardens, where space was limited and growing conditions were less than ideal for growing grass. Briggs also employed ground covers as a means of delineating a garden's design or to maintain established shapes and forms. Briggs often used the following ground covers in his designs:

Briggs relied on ornamental plants that offered maximum spring bloom, as shown in this Tradd Street garden designed for Mrs. Frederick Richards.

English ivy

Daylily

Liriope

Fig vine

Right: Carolina jessamine

BOTANICAL NAME	COMMON NAME/NAMES	PLACE OF ORIGIN
Aspidistra elatior	cast-iron plant	China
Hedera helix	English ivy	Europe
Hemerocallis 'Hyperion'	daylily	North America
Liriope muscari	liriope	China and Japan
Vinca major	bigleaf periwinkle	England
Vinca minor	common periwinkle	England

Vines

Vines include a variety of evergreen and deciduous plants that derive their support by climbing, twining, or attaching themselves by roots or tendrils to walls, fences, gates, and trellises. Vines play an important role in small gardens because of their ability to soften walls and fences. Vines also can be used to embellish garden features such as gates, columns, balconies, and porches. Of equal importance is the ability of vines to create shade when trained on arbors, pergolas, or trellises. Many vines add visual interest to a garden by providing seasonal color, leaf texture, flowers, fruit, and fragrance. In selecting vines for use in Charleston gardens, Briggs relied on both native and exotic species, as indicated in the selections below:

BOTANICAL NAME	COMMON NAME/NAMES	PLACE OF ORIGIN
Antigonon leptopus	coral vine	Central America
Ficus pumila	fig vine	China
Gelsemium sempervirens	Carolina jessamine	southeastern U.S.
Smilax lanceolata	southern smilax	eastern U.S.
Trachelospermum jasminoides	star jasmine, Confederate jasmine	China and Japan
Wisteria sinensis	wisteria	China

Star jasmine

Sweet shrub

Small Shrubs

Small shrubs generally grow from one to four feet tall. These versatile plants are particularly useful in gardens of limited space as they provide structure and definition to a design. In selecting appropriate small shrubs for Charleston gardens, Briggs chose those with distinctive characteristics such as evergreen foliage, decorative fruit, fragrant flowers, or the ability to be clipped into formal shapes or hedges. An additional consideration included shrubs that could tolerate the heat and humidity of Charleston summers. Small shrubs that Briggs particularly favored for use in Charleston gardens included the following selections:

BOTANICAL NAME	COMMON NAME/NAMES	PLACE OF ORIGIN
Azalea obtusum	Kurume azalea	Japan
Buxus microphylla var. *japonica*	Japanese box	Europe and Asia
Buxus harlandii	Harland box	Europe
Calycanthus floridus	sweet shrub	southeastern U.S.
Cleyera japonica	cleyera	Japan
Gardenia jasminoides	gardenia	China and Japan
Illicium parviflorum	anise	southeastern U.S.
Nandina domestica	nandina	China
Philadelphus coronarius	mock orange	southern Europe
Yucca filamentosa	Adam's needle	southeastern U.S.

Large Shrubs

Large shrubs reach an average height of six to ten feet in size. Those that are evergreen in nature are particularly useful for screening and background plantings or as a single specimen to create a special effect or serve as a focal point. Briggs carefully selected large shrubs based on their individual

Mock orange

Nandina

Oleander

Tea olive

Azalea

BOTANICAL NAME	COMMON NAME/NAMES	PLACE OF ORIGIN
Nerium oleander	oleander	southern Europe
Osmanthus fragrans	tea olive	China and Japan
Pittosporum tobira	pittosporum	China and Japan
Podocarpus macrophylla	Japanese yew	Japan
Prunus caroliniana	cherry laurel	southeastern U.S.
Viburnum tinus	laurustinus	southern Europe

Small Trees

Small trees generally reach an average height of twenty to thirty feet. Because of their limited size, they are used less for shade than to provide seasonal interest through the display of flowers, fruits, and foliage. Small trees can be upright or spreading in nature. In addition to their aesthetic qualities, small trees also provide scale to a garden. Small trees appropriate for Charleston's walled gardens include selections that will grow in limited space and remain proportionate to the size of the garden. Briggs used the following small trees in Charleston's small gardens:

character, growth habit, and ability to conform to the constraints of limited space. Large shrubs are usually planted in the rear of a garden to form a backdrop for smaller shrubs in the foreground. Briggs traditionally used the following large shrubs in Charleston's walled gardens:

BOTANICAL NAME	COMMON NAME/NAMES	PLACE OF ORIGIN
Azalea indica	Chinese azalea	China
Camellia japonica	camellia	China and Japan
Camellia sasanqua	sasanqua	China and Japan
Ilex vomitoria	yaupon holly	southeastern U.S.
Ligustrum japonica	wax-leaf ligustrum	Japan
Michelia figo	banana shrub	China

BOTANICAL NAME	COMMON NAME/NAMES	PLACE OF ORIGIN
Cercis canadensis	redbud	eastern and central U.S.
Cornus florida	flowering dogwood	eastern U.S.
Eriobotrya japonica	loquat	China and Japan
Lagerstroemia indica	crape myrtle	China
Magnolia virginiana	sweetbay magnolia	eastern U.S.
Vitex agnus-castus	chaste tree	Mediterranean region

Chaste tree

Loquat

Sweetbay magnolia

Overleaf: Southern magnolia

Large Trees

Large trees include a wide range of evergreen and deciduous species that vary in height, trunk size, branching habit, and leaf size. Because of their imposing size, large trees must be carefully selected to fit within the space limitations of a small garden. In instances where shade is desired in a small garden, the location, size, and placement of a large tree is critical to the success of the garden's design. In some instances a large tree, such as an evergreen magnolia, may be employed to screen an unsightly view or to soften the visual impact of an adjoining wall or building. In situations where a large tree exists on a site before a garden is planned, it has the potential of being integrated into the overall design of the garden. While Briggs seldom recommended the use of large trees in Charleston's small gardens, he occasionally used the following to address special needs:

BOTANICAL NAME	COMMON NAME/NAMES	PLACE OF ORIGIN
Magnolia grandiflora	southern magnolia	southeastern U.S.
Quercus phellos	willow oak	southeastern U.S.
Quercus virginiana	live oak	southeastern U.S.

Annuals

Annuals are flowering plants that survive for only one season. By employing a selection of both winter and summer annuals, it is possible to achieve seasonal color in Charleston gardens throughout the year. Long prized for their colorful blooms, annuals are indispensable in small gardens, where they can be grown in pots, planters, window boxes, or flower beds. Charleston's mild winters make the planting of winter annuals—such as English daisies, pansies, and snapdragons—ideal for city gardens. In spring Charleston gardeners rely on spring and summer annuals—including larkspur, calendula, and stock—that last well into May and June.

BOTANICAL NAME	COMMON NAME/NAMES	PLACE OF ORIGIN
Antirrhinum majus	snapdragon	Mediterranean region
Bellis perennis	English daisy	Britain
Calendula officinalis	calendula	southern Europe
Delphinium consolida	larkspur	North America
Matthiola incana	stock	Britain
Viola tricola var. *hortensis*	pansy	Europe

Perennials

Perennials are herbaceous plants that flower in the spring or summer, die back in fall and winter, and return the following year. As perennials

Snapdragon

Calendula

English daisies and pansies

survive for many years, it is important that the soil be carefully prepared to accommodate a large root system. While prized for their bright and colorful flowers, perennials seldom bloom as long and prolifically as annuals. Because perennials perform best in sunny locations, they have limited use in Charleston gardens except those that can tolerate shade.

BOTANICAL NAME	COMMON NAME/NAMES	PLACE OF ORIGIN
Cyrtomium falcatum	holly fern	China and Japan
Hedychium coronarium	ginger lily	Asia
Iberis sempervirens	candytuft	Europe
Iris germanica	bearded iris	early American hybrids
Phlox subulata	moss pink	North America

Holly fern

Iris

A Cherokee rose enhances an old wall in a Charleston garden in spring.

Roses

Roses have been grown in Charleston gardens since the earliest of times. In 1811 John Champneys, a Charleston rice planter, crossed the China rose 'Old Blush' with a white musk rose to create 'Champneys' Pink Cluster'—the first rose to be hybridized in America. When Loutrel Briggs first visited Charleston in 1927, he found roses growing in many Charleston gardens. Of particular interest were the Cherokee and Lady Banks roses, both of which provide spectacular displays as they cover old garden walls and cascade over porches and piazzas in spring. In addition to these traditional favorites, Briggs also employed newer hybrids in many of his garden plans.

BOTANICAL NAME	COMMON NAME/NAMES	PLACE OF ORIGIN
Rosa banksiae	Lady Banks rose	China
Rosa laevigata	Cherokee rose	China
Rosa hybrids	hybrid rose	Europe and North America

Cherokee rose

Lady Banks rose

Right: Hybrid rose

Appendix 1

Garden Easements

A Brief Overview

ERIC REISMAN, HISTORIC PRESERVATION PROFESSIONAL

Many garden owners, especially those with gardens of unique design or historic significance, are faced with the dilemma of how to preserve their gardens once they are no longer able to care for them. There are a variety of measures for ensuring that a garden is preserved beyond the gardener's lifetime. One of the first options a garden owner should consider is a garden easement.

A garden easement is a subcategory of a conservation easement, a voluntary legal agreement between a landowner and another party that is created for protecting the property's natural or historic value. As a voluntary legal agreement, such an easement provides a legal means for a concerned property owner to ensure that his or her property is maintained and protected for posterity in accordance with his or her wishes. Conservation easements may be created through sale or donation and are typically held by either government agencies or nonprofit organizations with 501(c)(3) status.

A garden easement "protects the historic and natural values of a man-made garden."[1] Garden easements, which incorporate attributes from conservation and historic preservation easements, have been in use for approximately twenty years.[2] Presently only a few organizations hold garden easements, and the number of gardens protected by them is small in comparison to the number of historic properties and open spaces thus encumbered. This is mainly owing to a general lack of awareness of the existence of garden easements and how to use them effectively.

Establishing Garden Easements

A garden owner who is interested in establishing a garden easement should carry out some background research on potential easement holders before initiating formal proceedings with receptive organizations. In particular a garden owner should make sure that prospective organizations are well established and qualified to hold and enforce an easement. In large part this can be determined by examining an organization's past successes in administrating and enforcing the easements that they hold.

A garden owner may donate an easement to either a governmental agency or a nonprofit organization with 501(c)(3) status. Most easements are donated to the latter, as government agencies generally use easement programs to pursue large-scale land conservation.[3] In contrast 501(c)(3) organizations such as historic foundations, land trusts, or garden clubs are often receptive to taking easements on gardens that are consistent with their agendas and missions.[4]

Garden easements may be sold or donated. Purchase of garden easements is not a common practice and is mainly carried out by government agencies.[5] Donation is the more common method and is preferred by the vast majority of nonprofits that hold garden easements, as these

A Briggs garden restored by the current owners in the spirit of its original design

organizations typically do not possess the means to purchase easements.[6]

Benefits of Garden Easements

There are many benefits to placing an easement on one's garden. An easement will protect a garden in perpetuity. Once recorded, an easement runs with the title to the land, legally obligating all future owners of the property to comply with the terms and conditions that are specified within the easement.[7]

Garden easements allow owners to protect their gardens while retaining their property. Prior to the use of garden easements, people who were truly interested in preserving their gardens had to sell or donate their land to individuals or organizations that were committed to maintaining the gardens in the future. With a garden easement, the owner retains possession of his or her land, along with the rights and responsibilities associated with property ownership, while the costs associated with long-term monitoring and enforcement of the easement are placed in the hands of the organization that holds the easement.[8]

Another benefit of easements is their versatility. Garden easements can easily be adapted to meet a wide variety of different circumstances.[9] Most easement-holding organizations understand that, when a person donates a garden easement, certain conditions may need to be met in order to satisfy the easement donor. Therefore organizations are flexible in tailoring the exact terms and conditions of an easement to suit the owner's wishes and protect the integrity of the garden.

Points to Consider before Donating an Easement

A garden easement is a legal contract, and there are many issues that a prospective donor should take into consideration prior to donating an easement. By taking the time to become familiar with potential requirements beforehand, the garden owner will make the process of donation easier and more satisfying for all concerned parties.

One important fact to remember is that a garden easement should provide some general public benefit. It is strongly recommended that a garden owner include a clause in the easement granting some public access to the garden. Many easement-holding organizations require just such a clause, and the federal government requires some public access in order for the owner to claim a tax deduction.[10] Typically having a garden that is viewable from the street is sufficient to meet the IRS requirement for public access.

It is the responsibility of the garden owner and any future owners to make sure that they completely understand the terms and conditions of the easement. While it is the responsibility of the buyer to be aware of the easement, ethically a seller should always inform a potential buyer of the existence of the easement and its stipulations.

Another item that should be taken into consideration is that one's property may potentially depreciate in value after donating a garden easement.[11] Fortunately any loss in property value may often be mitigated through judicious use of the federal and state tax incentives that exist for charitable donations.

A garden owner should donate only to an organization that has the human and financial resources to monitor and enforce the terms of an easement. Easement holding is a significant long-term responsibility, and many easement-holding organizations require a one-time "monitoring fee"

to be paid when the easement is donated. The amount of this fee will vary and can be anywhere from a nominal amount of money to more than several thousand dollars.

An easement should be worded in a way that clearly defines the rights and responsibilities of the garden owner and the easement-holding organization.[12] A key element of thoroughly documenting a garden involves the creation of a baseline document, which consists of a detailed description of the important cultural and historic attributes of the garden at the time when the easement is conveyed, along with recommendations for future maintenance.[13] Baseline documentation is a particularly crucial component of the easement, as the information contained within it will help to provide legal recourse in the event that the easement holder should have to go to court to have the provisions of the easement upheld. For most gardens baseline documentation will consist of a written description of the garden's history and existing conditions, as well as a wide variety of visual media such as maps, drawings, and photographs, the purpose of which is to create a detailed record of the garden's aesthetic, cultural, and horticultural values at the time the easement is granted.

When donating an easement, one should always seek guidance from qualified professionals. Easements should be prepared by lawyers with specific expertise on easement laws in the state where the garden is located.

Financial Benefits of Easement Donation

A garden owner who donates an easement to a government entity or a nonprofit organization may be entitled to federal, state, and local property-tax incentives. These incentives were created as a means of encouraging conservation efforts by recognizing the resulting decrease in property value that may result from easement donation.

If the garden owner intends to claim federal or state tax benefits, it is important to employ the services of a licensed appraiser, who can precisely assess the value of the charitable contribution.

As the logistics of claiming a charitable deduction are often complex, it pays to employ the services of an accountant who is particularly knowledgeable about such tax deductions.

Income Tax

A garden owner who donates an easement may be eligible to claim the easement value as a federal income-tax deduction. The IRS considers garden easements to be "qualified conservation contributions," provided that a real-property interest is conveyed in perpetuity, donated to an organization qualified to assume the easement, and given exclusively for conservation purposes.[14]

In addition the IRS requires a baseline document to be prepared in order to claim a tax deduction.[15] For most gardens, this consists of a written description of the garden's history and existing conditions, augmented by a wide variety of visual media such as photographs, maps, and drawings in order to create a detailed record of the garden's aesthetic, cultural, and horticultural values at the time that the easement is granted.

Typically the value of the easement is calculated to be the difference between the values of the property before and after it has been encumbered by an easement. The easement value should be obtained by a qualified appraiser, as the IRS has been quick to inflict significant penalties for carelessly overvalued easements. Under present law, a maximum of 50 percent of one's contribution base may be deducted for "qualified conservation contributions." Any remaining easement value that cannot be claimed on the initial return may be claimed within the next fifteen successive tax returns. Unless extended by an act of Congress, these provisions are set to expire on December 31, 2010, whereupon a maximum of 30 percent of one's contribution base may be deducted, which can be carried over for five years. Other external expenses associated with easement donation, such as accounting, appraisal, and legal fees can also be deducted.

In addition to the federal tax benefits, many states also offer tax incentives for garden-easement donation, which may be claimed in conjunction with the federal tax deductions. To find out if your state offers tax incentives, contact your state department of revenue.

Estate Tax

Many owners of large or lavishly designed gardens may find that their gardens are of a sufficient value to raise their net worth to a level high enough to trigger the estate tax. Currently the IRS allows owners of land subject to a garden easement to exempt 40 percent of the encumbered land's value from the estate tax. Therefore, by donating an easement on one's garden, a taxpayer may reduce his or her net worth to a level where the estate tax is no longer applicable.

Since the passage of the Economic Growth and Tax Reconciliation Act (EGTRRA) in 2001, the amount of one's estate subject to the estate tax has gradually been reduced. However, EGTRRA is set to expire in 2011, whereupon the estate tax will be reinstated at a rate of 55 percent on all estates in excess of one million dollars.[16] This change will dramatically increase the number of estates eligible for taxation, making garden easements a potentially useful tool to reduce one's taxes.

Gift Taxes

Under current IRS code, annual gifts up to twelve thousand dollars are exempt from the gift tax. This amount can be doubled to twenty-four thousand dollars if the gift is made by a married couple filing a joint return. There is no limit to the number of recipients that a donor may give to in a single year. In addition to the annual limits, the IRS permits a taxpayer to exempt an additional one million dollars in gifts over his or her lifetime.

Although donating a garden easement in itself does not exempt garden owners from the gift tax, an easement may reduce the value of a garden to the point where, if a garden owner decides to make a gift of his or her garden, the gift tax will no longer be applicable. In addition, by gradually giving a garden of significant value to another party, a garden owner has the opportunity to transfer ownership of the garden to a desired recipient without being subject to gift taxes.

Property Taxes

On donating an easement, most garden owners will be entitled to a property-tax reassessment. State and local laws concerning reassessment of properties encumbered by easements vary. Some states require an automatic reassessment for cultural easements, while others place the impetus for a reappraisal in the hands of the property owner. Many local tax assessors are unfamiliar with their state's laws concerning easement valuation, making it even more imperative that the easement donor be knowledgeable of his or her state's laws. It is advisable to contact one's local tax assessor's office prior to donating an easement.

While a revised appraisal will typically result in a lower property value and a correspondingly lower property-tax assessment, this outcome is by no means certain. In instances where the unencumbered portion of a property has dramatically increased in value, a reassessment may actually result in a property-tax increase. The flexibility of garden easements—combined with their financial advantages and long-term legal strength—should ensure that garden easements become a permanent legal tool for the preservation of significant gardens in the United States.

Notes

1. Eric Reisman, "The Use of Garden Easements to Protect Gardens of Historical and Cultural Significance (master's thesis, University of Georgia, 2009), 35.

2. The Garden Conservancy, "Preservation Project Gardens: The Ruth Bancroft Garden, Walnut Creek, Calif.," available at http://www.gardenconservancy.org/presGard.pl?ID=11 (accessed June 2, 2008). The Ruth Bancroft Garden, in Walnut Creek, California, was placed under an easement in 1989 and is generally regarded as the first private garden to be protected in this way.

3. Elizabeth Byers and Karin Marchetti Ponte, *The Conservation Easement Handbook,* 2nd ed. (Washington, D.C.: Land Trust Alliance / San Francisco: Trust for Public Land, 2005), 241. Government agencies generally utilize conservation easements to encumber large tracts of farmland, open spaces, or forest to prevent these areas from being developed.

4. Ibid., 246–48.

5. Ibid., 245.

6. Garden Conservancy, *The Garden Conservancy Conservation Easement Program: Guides for the Owner* (pamphlet, n.d.), 3.

7. Richard Brewer, *Conservancy: The Land Trust Movement in America* (Lebanon, N.H.: University Press of New England, 2003), 2.

8. See Samuel N. Stokes, Elizabeth A. Watson, and Shelly S. Mastran, *Saving America's Countryside: A Guide to Rural Conservation,* 2nd ed. (Baltimore: Johns Hopkins University Press, 1997), 226–28, for a thorough description of the garden owner's rights and those of the easement-holding organization.

9. Sally K. Fairfax and Darla Guenzler, *Conservation Trusts* (Lawrence: University Press of Kansas, 2001), 125.

10. See U.S. Internal Revenue Code 170(h)(4): "Conservation Purpose Defined."

11. Brewer, *Conservancy,* 146.

12. Christopher Todd Fullerton, "The Use of Cultural Easements for the Protection of Historic Resources in Georgia" (master's thesis, University of Georgia, 2004), 46.

13. Garden Conservancy, *The Garden Conservancy Conservation Easement Program,* 21. If a garden is particularly complex, it might be advisable to create a separate management plan exclusively devoted to the proper treatment of a garden's component features.

14. U.S. Internal Revenue Code 170(h)(1).

15. Garden Conservancy, *The Garden Conservancy Conservation Easement Program,* 21.

16. See U.S. Internal Revenue Code 2031(c).

Appendix 2
Garden Easement Resources

Throughout the United States there are nonprofit organizations with 501(c)(3) status that are eligible to accept the donation of garden easements. Garden easements not only provide potential financial benefits but also preserve the historic or design integrity of a garden in perpetuity. To ensure that a garden easement is enforced, periodic monitoring of an easement is provided by the holding agency/organization, based on a one time initial fee.

Nonprofit Organizations in Charleston

Charleston, South Carolina, has two such organizations. Trained staffs are available at each to provide guidance on the technicalities and potential financial benefits garden easements. For additional information on garden easements, contact the following organizations:

Historic Charleston Foundation
40 East Bay Street
Charleston, S.C. 29401
Telephone: 843.723.1623
www.historiccharleston.com

Preservation Society of Charleston
147 King Street
Charleston, S.C. 29401
Telephone: 843.722.4630
preserve@preservationsociety.org

Organizations Outside Charleston

Many towns and cities throughout the United States have organizations similar to those in Charleston, offering opportunities for the donation of garden easements. To determine if such organizations exist in a particular location, one should contact the following:

Local or regional preservation organizations or land trusts with 501(c)(3) status:

State Historic Preservation Office

The National Trust for Historic Preservation
1785 Massachusetts Avenue N.W.
Washington, D.C. 20036-2117
Telephone: 202.588.6000

The Garden Conservancy
P.O. Box 219
Cold Spring, New York 10516
Telephone: 845.265.2029
www.gardenconservancy.org

Individuals may also contact the following organizations:

The Cultural Landscape Foundation
1909 Q Street N.W.
Second Floor
Washington, D.C. 20009
Phone: 202.483.0553

American Society of Landscape Architects
636 I Street, N.W.
Washington, D.C. 20001-3736
Phone: 202.898.2444

Appendix 3

Documentation of Briggs' Gardens

Within recent years many of Loutrel Briggs' Charleston gardens have been lost because of poor maintenance, redesign, natural disasters, or change of ownership. Recognizing the loss of these historic resources, the Historic Charleston Foundation—in concert with Atlanta landscape architect James Cothran, FASLA—sponsored an educational workshop at the foundation's headquarters in the spring of 2003 to explore the possibility of initiating a project directed at inventorying and documenting Briggs' Charleston gardens.

Historic preservation students from the College of Charleston using resources from the archives of the Historic Charleston Foundation to document a Briggs garden

Guidelines for the federal program to document cultural landscapes

Volunteers under the direction of Charleston landscape architect Glen Gardner preparing to document a Briggs garden

To undertake this ambitious effort, the Historic Charleston Foundation, the Charleston Preservation Society of Charleston, the Charleston Horticultural Society, and the South Carolina Historical Society formed a coalition. Staff and volunteers from these organizations documented numerous Briggs gardens. Material developed from the project is housed in the archives of the Historic Charleston Foundation and is available to property owners, landscape architects, garden historians, and the general public. It is hoped that this material will assist in preserving and restoring Briggs' Charleston gardens.

The Briggs garden-documentation project was carried out in concert with the Historic American Landscapes Survey (HALS) initiative—a national program established in 2000 as a collaboration of the National Park Service, the American Society of Landscape Architects, and the Library of Congress to document cultural landscapes. While the Briggs garden project does not meet the established standards of the HALS documentation effort, it does serve as a model for employing local volunteers and limited resources to complement the HALS initiative. For information regarding the Briggs garden project contact:

Historic Charleston Foundation
40 East Bay Street
Charleston, South Carolina 29401
Telephone: 843.723.1623
www.historiccharleston.org

Appendix 4

Loutrel Briggs Archives

South Carolina Historical Society and Historic Charleston Foundation

Archival material relating to Loutrel Briggs' landscape architectural practice is housed at the South Carolina Historical Society and the Historic Charleston Foundation. Each of the collections includes a wide range of plans and drawings of projects Briggs completed during his prolific career as a landscape architect. Of the two collections, the largest and most comprehensive is housed at the South Carolina Historical Society. Founded in 1855, the South Carolina Historical Society, located at 100 Meeting Street in Charleston, South Carolina), is the states' oldest and largest private repository of books, letters, journals, maps, drawings, and photographs relating to Charleston and South Carolina history. The following is a brief description of archival material contained in the Briggs collection at the South Carolina Historical Society:

> Briggs, Loutrel W., 1893–1977.
> Records. 1919–1974. 1,065 items
> Landscape architect, landscape architectural historian and author of *Charleston Gardens.* Measured drawings, blueprints, sketches, and finished drawings for approximately 300 clients in Calif., Conn., Fla., Ga., La., Mass., N.H., N.J., N.Y., Pa., S.C., Tenn., and the District of Columbia. The majority of the designs are for projects in S.C., often in Charleston, where Briggs spent winters from 1927, working at, among other places, 39 E. Battery, 94 Rutledge, 58 Church, 23 Meeting Streets, Robt. Mills Manor, College of Charleston and The Citadel. Other places in S.C. where he did work include Hartsville (Coker Estate), Lake City (Wannamaker Estate), Spartanburg, and Sumter. He

also worked on plantations and estates in Berkeley Co. (Mepkin, Mulberry and Yeamans Hall), Georgetown Co. (Chicora Wood and Exchange) and elsewhere. Types of jobs include urban gardens, suburban estates, plantation gardens, commercial landscaping, school grounds, government housing projects, cemeteries, and subdivision plans. Types of details include site plans, building elevations, wall designs, etc. Included in this collection are general plans by the Olmsted Brothers of Brookline, Mass., for the Yeamans Hall Club (Berkeley Co.), 1925, and "The Crescent" subdivision (Charleston), 1926.
> Gift of John David Utterback, 1980.

Additional archival material documenting significant examples of Briggs' work is housed at the Historic Charleston Foundation, located at 40 East Bay Street. Founded in 1947 to preserve and protect the integrity of Charleston's architectural, historical, and cultural heritage, the Historic Charleston Foundation seeks to achieve its objective through advocacy programs, participation in community planning, innovative educational programs, the preservation of historic properties, technical and financial assistance, and the collection and dissemination of historic resource material. While the Briggs collection at the Historic Charleston Foundation is less extensive than the collection at the South Carolina Historical Society, it documents some of the earliest and most significant projects Briggs carried out shortly after opening a seasonal office in Charleston in 1929. Included in the collection are plans for the garden of the William Gibbes House, along with landscape drawings of Rice Hope, Mulberry, and

Historic photograph of the Washington Roebling garden at 64 South Battery

Mepkin plantations. Each of these projects is a significant example of work Briggs completed in the late 1920s and early 1930s. The collection also includes recent documentation (beginning in 2003) of numerous Briggs' gardens, including current owners and conditions.

While the archival collections at the South Carolina Historical Society and the Historic Charleston Foundation include a wide range of Briggs material—including plans, drawings, historic photographs, and narrative material—the collections do not include all the projects Briggs completed during his career, especially projects in the North. Even so the collections reflect Briggs' expertise and versatile talents as one of America's most prolific and talented twentieth-century landscape architects.

The only known drawings of projects completed by Loutrel Briggs in the northeastern United States are in the archives of the South Carolina Historical Society and the Historic Charleston Foundation. It is hoped that additional material will surface in the future, offering greater insight into Briggs' life and career.

Loutrel Briggs' Archives at the South Carolina Historical Society

REF. NO.	ORIGINAL OWNER / LOCATION	AVAILABLE INFORMATION
1.	Mr. and Mrs. James R. Adams 18 Yeamans Road—The Crescent Charleston, S.C.	design of grounds
2.	Dr. and Mrs. Julian C. Adams No. 1728 Hollywood Columbia, S.C. March 2, 1972	garden design
3.	Dr. and Mrs. H. H. Addlestone Charleston, S.C. February 21, 1949	sketch plan
4.	George Marshall Allen, Esq. Fort Lauderdale, Fla. no date	sketch of a garden house
5.	Applegate Charleston, S.C. no date	plan of drive and patio
6.	Archdale Road and Jamestown Road no date	site plan with field notes
7.	Ashelawn Garden of Memory, Inc. Asheville, N.C. July 2, 1958	garden of devotion
8.	Dormitory building for Ashley Hall Charleston, S.C. no date	construction drawings
9.	61 Ashley Avenue Charleston, S.C. no date	old-time garden
10.	Ashley Hall Charleston, S.C. 1770 (del. 1948)	plan of gardens and grounds
11.	Ashley Hall Charleston, S.C. December 1948	plan of gardens and grounds
12.	Ashley Hall School Charleston, S.C. April 10, 1958	preliminary plan, campus development with field notes
13.	Ashley Hall School Charleston, S.C. November 6, 1959	construction drawing, forecourt to dormitory
14.	Ashley Hall School Charleston, S.C. April 10, 1958	preliminary plan, campus development

REF. NO.	ORIGINAL OWNER / LOCATION	AVAILABLE INFORMATION
15.	Ashley River bridge approach Charleston, S.C. March 4, 1955	planting plan for no. 1 park
16.	Ashley River bridge approach Charleston, S.C. March 8, 1955	planting plan for no. 1 park
17.	Ashley River bridge approach Charleston, S.C. April 2, 1954	plan for a riverside park and bird sanctuary
18.	Ashley River bridge approach Charleston, S.C. January 27, 1954	plat showing city owned property
19.	Commander and Mrs. Alfred W. Atkins 42 South Battery Charleston, S.C. February 20, 1934	details of garden
20.	Howard Auerbach White Plains, N.Y. no date	lattice
21.	E. B. Aymar, Esq. Bronxville, N.Y. July 18, 1922	lattice for drying yard and garden
22.	Mrs. Barbara C. Ayres 1 Battery Place Charleston, S.C. January 20, 1971	construction plan—garden
23.	Mrs. Barbara C. Ayres 1 Battery Place Charleston, S.C. November 2, 1970	construction plan, garden with field notes
24.	Mrs. Barbara C. Ayres 1 Battery Place Charleston, S.C. December 10, 1970	planting plan
25.	Mrs. Barbara C. Ayres 1 Battery Place Charleston, S.C. December 10, 1970	planting plan
26.	Mr. and Mrs. F. H. Bailey 12 Lamboll Street Charleston, S.C. October 26, 1967	redesign of garden
27.	Mr. and Mrs. F. H. Bailey 12 Lamboll Street Charleston, S.C. October 26, 1967	redesign of garden

REF. NO.	ORIGINAL OWNER / LOCATION	AVAILABLE INFORMATION
28.	Mr. and Mrs. F. H. Bailey 12 Lamboll Street Charleston, S.C. March 27, 1967	plan of paving
29.	Mr. and Mrs. Ronald S. Banks Summerville, S.C. June 21, 1970	masonry plan
30.	Mr. and Mrs. Wm. H. Barnwell 42 Legare Street Charleston, S.C. March 1957	garden plan
31.	Mr. Lockwood Barr Pelham Manor, N.Y. September 1928	planting plan of garden
32.	Mrs. Ward C. Belcher Horse Branch Hall Camden, S.C. no date	additions to garden
33.	Mrs. Edna M. Bitzer Woodbrook Estates Doylestown, Pa. November 10, 1953	drive profiles
34.	Mrs. Edna M. Bitzer Woodbrook Estates Doylestown, Pa. November 10, 1953	preliminary plan of subdivision
35.	Raymond D. Bitzer Doylestown, Pa. June 23, 1953	copy of boundary survey
36.	Raymond D. Bitzer Doylestown, Pa. June 23, 1953	contour plan of a farm
37.	Raymond D. Bitzer and Edna M. Bitzer Doylestown, Pa. September 3, 1953	preliminary plan no. 2, subdivision
38.	Raymond D. Bitzer and Edna M. Bitzer Doylestown, Pa. September 3, 1953	preliminary plan no. 2, subdivision
39.	Mr. and Mrs. G. R. Blanton Summerville, S.C. December 30, 1947	garden plan
40.	Mrs. G. D. B. Bonbright Pimlico February 25, 1930	sketch of gate and wall

REF. NO.	ORIGINAL OWNER / LOCATION	AVAILABLE INFORMATION
41.	Mrs. C. E. Boyd 55½ Legare Street Charleston, S.C. February 27, 1952	lattice
42.	Mrs. C. E. Boyd 55½ Legare Street Charleston, S.C. February 27, 1952	garden plan
43.	Ann Clare Brokaw Mepkin, S.C. August 22, 1924	headstone inscription
44.	Bucks County Historical Society Doylestown Bucks County, Pa. April 1, 1943	contour plan with field notes
45.	Bucks County Historical Society Doylestown Bucks County, Pa. April 1, 1943	rendered preliminary sketch plan
46.	Bucks County, Pa. 1948	map of the public roads
47.	Bucks County Historical Society Doylestown Bucks County, Pa. May 2, 1950	general plan of grounds
48.	Bucks County Historical Society Doylestown Bucks County, Pa. May 2, 1950	general plan of grounds
49.	Bridgewater Township Somerset County, N.J. August 1934	map of property
50.	L. W. Briggs Doylestown, Pa. November 18, 1944	study no. 3, building made from four shipping crates
51.	Mr. and Mrs. L. W. Briggs 3 Ladson Street Charleston, S.C. August 1, 1958	construction details of house
52.	Mr. and Mrs. L. W. Briggs 3 Ladson Street Charleston, S.C. August 1, 1958	elevations of house
53.	Mr. and Mrs. L. W. Briggs (2 copies) 3 Ladson Street Charleston, S.C. August 1, 1958	interior elevations

REF. NO.	ORIGINAL OWNER / LOCATION	AVAILABLE INFORMATION
54.	Mr. and Mrs. L. W. Briggs 3 Ladson Street Charleston, S.C. August 1, 1958	plans of residence
55.	L. W. Briggs 89 Church Street Charleston, S.C. August 20, 1935	pantry
56.	L. W. Briggs 89 Church Street Charleston, S.C. September 10, 1954	extension to south house
57.	L. W. Briggs 3 Ladson Street Charleston, S.C. March 9, 1959	plan of grounds
58.	Mr. and Mrs. L. W. Briggs 3 Ladson Street Charleston, S.C. August 1, 1958	plans of residence
59.	Mr. and Mrs. L. W. Briggs (9) 3 Ladson Street Charleston, S.C. August 1, 1958	plans of residence
60.	L. W. Briggs (2) 3 Ladson Street Charleston, S.C. November 3, 1958	air conditioning and heating
61.	Mr. and Mrs. Loutrel W. Briggs Princeton, N.J. January 20, 1954	residence, J. Floyd Yewell, architect (11 sheets)
62.	Mr. and Mrs. Loutrel W. Briggs Newlin Road Princeton, N.J. May 6, 1954	site plan
63.	Mr. and Mrs. Loutrel W. Briggs Princeton, N.J. June 29, 1964	kitchen details and l.r. bookcases
64.	Mr. and Mrs. Loutrel W. Briggs Princeton, N.J. May 18, 1954	complete alterations of end f/r plan
65.	L. W. Briggs, property of Doylestown, Pa. no date	site plan
66.	L. W. Briggs High Hampton, N.C. January 10, 1962	grading—drive drainage

REF. NO.	ORIGINAL OWNER / LOCATION	AVAILABLE INFORMATION
67.	Mr. and Mrs. Loutrel W. Briggs (3) Cashiers, N.C. February 20, 1962	residence
68.	Mr. and Mrs. Loutrel W. Briggs (3) Cashiers, N.C. February 20, 1962	residence with field notes
69.	L. W. Briggs July 16, 1962	sketch showing modifications
70.	Mr. and Mrs. Raymond Brooks Greenwich, Conn.	sketch of garden
71.	Mr. Robert A. Burdick Mill Neck, L.I., N.Y. June 26, 1951	planting plan
72.	Mr. John Burling White Plains, N.Y. April 20, 1931	detail of picket fence
73.	Mrs. Felicia Candela Stepling Ridge Harrison, N.Y. no date	general plan of grounds at Muralta
74.	Mr. and Mrs. Norman L. Cannon 15 Lamboll Street Charleston, S.C. March 22, 1955	construction plan of garden
75.	Mr. and Mrs. Norman L. Cannon 15 Lamboll Street Charleston, S.C. December 12, 1955	planting plan for garden
76.	Mrs. R. C. Carmel Nutley, N.J. October 1, 1930	details of gate
77.	Carolina Academy Lake City, S.C. June 6, 1970	elevations
78.	Civic Services Committee Carolina Art Association Charleston, S.C. December 19, 1944	suggested layout for off-street parking facilities
79.	Miss Sallie C. Carrington Church Street Charleston, S.C. no date	garden pool
80.	Miss Sallie C. Carrington No. 7 Church Street Charleston, S.C. February 12, 1965	construction plan, walls and paving

REF. NO.	ORIGINAL OWNER / LOCATION	AVAILABLE INFORMATION
81.	Miss Sallie C. Carrington No. 7 Church Street Charleston, S.C. March 8, 1948	plan of garden
82.	Dr. Patricia A. Carter 203 Sans Souci Street Charleston, S.C. March 3, 1949	planting plan
83.	Mr. and Mrs. Alexander J. Cassatt 37-39 E. Battery Charleston, S.C. March 30, 1972	planting plan
84.	Mr. and Mrs. Alexander J. Cassatt 37-39 E. Battery Charleston, S.C. March 31, 1971	preliminary planting plan of garden
85.	Mr. and Mrs. Alexander J. Cassatt 37-39 E. Battery Charleston, S.C. May 11, 1971	steps to house and garden with field notes
86.	Mr. and Mrs. Alexander J. Cassatt 37-39 E. Battery Charleston, S.C. June 25, 1971	steps to house and garden
87.	Mr. and Mrs. Alexander J. Cassatt 37-39 E. Battery Charleston, S.C. May 11, 1971	steps to house and garden
88.	Mr. and Mrs. Alexander J. Cassatt 37-39 E. Battery Charleston, S.C. December 3, 1971	pool, exposed aggregate walk, and irrigation plan
89.	Mr. and Mrs. Alexander J. Cassatt 37-39 E. Battery Charleston, S.C. May 11, 1971	steps to house and garden
90.	Mr. and Mrs. Alexander J. Cassatt 37-39 E. Battery Charleston, S.C. May 31, 1971	construction plan of garden
91.	Mr. and Mrs. Alexander J. Cassatt 37-39 E. Battery Charleston, S.C. October 4, 1971	planting plan
92.	Catfish Row Charleston, S.C. November 1, 1934	north house and south house plans with suggested alterations

REF. NO.	ORIGINAL OWNER / LOCATION	AVAILABLE INFORMATION
93.	Mr. Joseph D. Ceader Riegelsville, Pa. June 29, 1949	construction details entrance and turn court
94.	Cemetery of the Immaculate Conception Mt. Hebron Road Montclair, N.J. no date	planting plan
95.	36 Chalmers Street Charleston, S.C. March 28, 1957	sketch of garden walk
96.	36 Chalmers Street Charleston, S.C. December 10, 1949	construction details of fountain
97.	Mr. Hugh Chapman 5033 Wittering Avenue Columbia, S.C. September 21, 1972	sketch plan
98.	Mrs. Clarence E. Chapman Mulberry Oakley, S.C. no date	details of seat on terrace
99.	Mrs. Clarence E. Chapman Welawiben Oakland, N.J. July 21, 1930	construction plan of garden
100.	Mrs. Clarence E. Chapman Welawiben Oakland, N.J. no date	details of south end of pool
101.	Mrs. Clarence E. Chapman Welawiben Oakland, N.J. September 12, 1930	construction details of pool
102.	Mrs. Clarence E. Chapman Welawiben Oakland, N.J. November 17, 1930	planting plan of pool garden
103.	Charleston Cemetery Charleston, S.C. August 4, 1956	gates by Henry P. Staats, architect
104.	Charleston Cemetery Charleston, S.C. July 30, 1956	tower and office sheets 1 and 2
105.	Office of City Engineer Charleston, S.C. 1954	map of streets

REF. NO.	ORIGINAL OWNER / LOCATION	AVAILABLE INFORMATION
106.	Charleston Housing Project site Charleston, S.C. December 9, 1935	site plan and diagram showing subsoil investigation
107.	Housing Authority City of Charleston, S.C. May 24, 1939	housing project, no. SC-1-3, details plumbing
108.	Housing Authority City of Charleston, S.C. October 30, 1940	planting plan, block 2, SC-1-6
109.	Housing Authority City of Charleston, S.C. October 30, 1940	planting plan, block 1, SC-1-6
110.	Housing Authority City of Charleston, S.C. December 15, 1938	planting plan for blocks 2 and 3, SC-1-1
111.	Housing Authority City of Charleston, S.C. December 14, 1938	planting plan for block 1, SC-1-1
112.	Housing Authority City of Charleston, S.C. December 15, 1938	planting plan for block 4, SC-1-1
113.	Housing Authority City of Charleston, S.C. January 9, 1935	general planting plan
114.	Housing Authority City of Charleston, S.C. May 17, 1940	housing project, no. SC-1-6, basement plans, types "A," "E" and "F"
115.	Housing Authority City of Charleston, S.C. October 29, 1938	housing project, no. SC-1-1, yard wall details, block 4
116.	Housing Authority City of Charleston, S.C. May 17, 1940	housing project, no. SC-1-6, entrance porch details, B-C-D-G
117.	Housing Authority City of Charleston, S.C. November 8, 1940	preliminary general landscape plan, project no. SC-1-7, sheet no. 801
118.	City parking lot Wentworth Street June 28, 1963	construction plan for walls
119.	City of Charleston Wentworth Street, St. Philip and Beaufain Street Charleston, S.C. October 10, 1956	parking-lot design

REF. NO.	ORIGINAL OWNER / LOCATION	AVAILABLE INFORMATION
120.	City of Charleston Wentworth Street, St. Philip and Beaufain Street Charleston, S.C. June 17, 1963	preliminary study
121.	City of Charleston Charleston, S.C. December 5, 1963	planting plan, sheet no. 3
122.	City of Charleston Wentworth Street, St. Philip and Beaufain Street Charleston, S.C. June 17, 1963	general plan, sheet no. 1
123.	City of Charleston Charleston, S.C. June 28, 1963	construction plan for walls, sheet no. 2
124.	City of Charleston Charleston, S.C. June 28, 1963	construction plan for walls, with field notes, sheet no. 2
125.	City of Charleston Wentworth Street, St. Philip and Beaufain Street Charleston, S.C. June 28, 1963	construction plan for walls, city parking lot
126.	City of Charleston Charleston, S.C. December 5, 1963	planting plan, city parking lot
127.	City of Charleston Charleston, S.C. June 17, 1963	general plan with field notes, sheet no. 1
128.	City Parks drawing, no. 2 February 14, 1929	gate details for garden club walk
129.	Charleston County Map S.C. 1942	details for fence and gates
130.	Charleston County Office Building Charleston, S.C. February 16, 1970	
131.	Charleston County Map Charleston, S.C. 1942	park
132.	Charleston County Office Building Charleston, S.C. June 7, 1967	exterior elevations

REF. NO.	ORIGINAL OWNER / LOCATION	AVAILABLE INFORMATION
133.	Charleston County Office Building (2) Charleston, S.C. June 7, 1967	site plan and details
134.	Charleston County Office Building Charleston, S.C. June 7, 1967	first-floor plan
135.	Charleston County Office Building Charleston, S.C. January 30, 1970	storm drainage revision, north side
136.	Charleston County T.B. Hospital, for the Garden Club of Charleston Charleston, S.C. February 8, 1955	planting plan no. 2 and recommended site improvements
137.	Charleston County T.B. Hospital, for the Garden Club of Charleston no location February 8, 1955	planting plan no. 2 and recommended site improvements
138.	Charleston County T.B. Hospital, for the Garden Club of Charleston no location January 26, 1955	planting plan no. 1
139.	Charleston County T.B. Hospital, for the Garden Club of Charleston no location January 26, 1955	planting plan no. 1
140.	The Charleston Garden Club S.C. Hall Charleston, S.C. no date	terrace
141.	The Charleston Garden Club S.C. Hall Charleston, S.C. no date	planting list
142.	The Charleston Garden Club S.C. Hall Charleston, S.C. December 30, 1952	plan for replanting of garden club
143.	The Charleston Garden Club S.C. Hall Charleston, S.C. December 30, 1952	construction plan for converting pool to a sunken garden
144.	The Charleston Garden Club S.C. Hall Charleston, S.C. no date	plan of rooms

REF. NO.	ORIGINAL OWNER / LOCATION	AVAILABLE INFORMATION
145.	Mrs. Henry Cheves III October 2, 1972	pool and fountain details—waterfall added
146.	Mr. Henry Cheves III 10 South Adgers Wharf Charleston, S.C. April 20, 1972	preliminary garden plan, swimming pool location
147.	Mr. Henry Cheves III 10 South Adgers Wharf Charleston, S.C. June 9, 1972	planting and construction plan of garden
148.	Mr. Henry Cheves III 10 South Adgers Wharf Charleston, S.C. April 20, 1972	preliminary garden plan, swimming pool location
149.	Mrs. Felix H. Chisolm Charleston, S.C. March 22, 1956	plan of garden
150.	Mrs. Felix H. Chisolm Charleston, S.C. March 22, 1956	plan of garden
151.	77 Church Street Charleston, S.C. March 20, 1946	plan of alterations
152.	Church Street Mt. Pleasant, S.C. December 1968	sketch of garden
153.	The Citadel Charleston, S.C. November 13, 1953	plot plan southwest quadrant
154.	The Citadel Charleston, S.C. June 14, 1954	general plan for site development, president's house
155.	The Citadel Charleston, S.C. June 14, 1954	general plan for site development, president's house
156.	The Citadel Charleston, S.C. February 5, 1954	proposed president's house, preliminary site plan
157.	The Citadel Charleston, S.C. October 30, 1956	campus layout
158.	The Citadel Charleston, S.C. October 20, 1954	planting plan for president's house

REF. NO.	ORIGINAL OWNER / LOCATION	AVAILABLE INFORMATION
159.	The Citadel Charleston, S.C. October 2, 1953	building program
160.	R. P. Clark, Esq. Bronxville, N.Y. no date	planting plan
161.	R. P. Clark, Esq. Bronxville, N.Y. no date	construction plan
162.	Dr. and Mrs. George H. A. Clowes, Jr. 122 Tradd Street Charleston, S.C. November 26, 1963	construction plan of garden
163.	The College of Charleston Charleston, S.C. March 22, 1956	recommended improvement of campus
164.	The College of Charleston Charleston, S.C. no date	college cistern and campus area with field notes
165.	Dormitory and student union The College of Charleston Charleston, S.C. May 25, 1961	site plan
166.	The College of Charleston Charleston, S.C. October 9, 1962	planting plan, dormitory and student union
167.	The College of Charleston Charleston, S.C. October 9, 1962	planting plan, dormitory and student union
168.	The College of Charleston Charleston, S.C. October 9, 1962	preliminary plan, dormitory and student union
169.	The College of Charleston 6 Glebe Street Charleston, S.C. September 1, 1966	preliminary site plan
170.	The College of Charleston 6 Glebe Street Charleston, S.C. April 12, 967	part of plan for garden
171.	The College of Charleston 6 Glebe Street Charleston, S.C. September 1, 1966	preliminary site plan

REF. NO.	ORIGINAL OWNER / LOCATION	AVAILABLE INFORMATION
172.	The College of Charleston 6 Glebe Street September 1, 1966	preliminary site (with planting notations)
173.	The College of Charleston Charleston, S.C. no date	planting at towers
174.	Alan C. Collins, Esq. Province Line Road Hopewell, N.J. November 12, 1955	plant location diagram, detail steps
175.	Colored Recreation Center Hartsville, S.C. December 7, 1944	preliminary drawings
176.	Housing project Columbia, S.C. no date	suggested details
177.	General and Mrs. Wm. Connor Tradd Street Charleston, S.C. April 1967	garden plan
178.	General and Mrs. Wm. Connor Tradd Street Charleston, S.C. December 27, 1966	garden plan
179.	Mr. and Mrs. C. W. Coker Hartsville, S.C. January 24, 1940	plan of border planting
180.	Mr. and Mrs. C. W. Coker Hartsville, S.C. January 24, 1940	plan of border planting
181.	Mr. and Mrs. C. W. Coker Hartsville, S.C. February 14, 1940	plan of alternate house and drive location
182.	Mr. and Mrs. Charles W. Coker Hartsville, S.C. January 9, 1946	design of garden
183.	Charles W. Coker, Jr. Hartsville, S.C. March 15, 1962	map of land and house location
184.	Mr. and Mrs. Charles W. Coker, Jr. Hartsville, S.C. April 6, 1962	general plan of grounds
185.	Charles W. Coker, Jr. no location July 31, 1962	contour map, elevations, trees on proposed house location

REF. NO.	ORIGINAL OWNER / LOCATION	AVAILABLE INFORMATION
186.	Mr. and Mrs. Charles W. Coker Hartsville, S.C. July 26, 1962	garden wall design
187.	Mr. and Mrs. Charles W. Coker, Jr. Hartsville, S.C. September 12, 1962	site plan
188.	Mr. and Mrs. Charles W. Coker, Jr. Hartsville, S.C. April 1932	general design of residence property
189.	Mr. and Mrs. J. L. Coker III Hartsville, S.C. December 17, 1936	general plan of garden
190.	Mr. and Mrs. J. L. Coker III Hartsville, S.C. April 6, 1937	construction details of garden
191.	Mr. and Mrs. J. L. Coker III Hartsville, S.C. April 9, 1937	plan of drive and garage court, detail of gate
192.	Mr. and Mrs. J. L. Coker III Hartsville, S.C. April 9, 1937	plan of drive and garage court, detail of gate
193.	Mr. and Mrs. J. L. Coker III Hartsville, S.C. December 16, 1959	construction drawing for drive and wall
194.	Mr. and Mrs. J. L. Coker III Hartsville, S.C. December 16, 1959	construction drawing for drive and wall
195.	Mr. and Mrs. J. L. Coker III Hartsville, S.C. October 16, 1959	plan no. 1 and plan no. 2, alternate plans of entrance court
196.	Mr. and Mrs. J. L. Coker III Hartsville, S.C. October 9, 1937	detail of gate posts
197.	Mr. and Mrs. J. L. Coker III Hartsville, S.C. October 16, 1959	plan no. 1 and plan no. 2
198.	J. L. Coker no date	fence detail
199.	J. L. Coker no date	fence detail
200.	J. L. Coker no date	south entrance to garden
201.	Coker Properties Hartsville, S.C. June 26, 1945	property plats

REF. NO.	ORIGINAL OWNER / LOCATION	AVAILABLE INFORMATION
202.	Coker Properties Hartsville, S.C. June 26, 1945	C. W. Coker house and drive location
203.	Mr. J. Walker Coleman, Jr. 5 Water Street Charleston, S.C. no date	planting and construction plan
204.	Mr. and Mrs. Walker Coleman, Jr. 5 Water Street Charleston, S.C. December 17, 1970	pool location
205.	Columbia Stone Co. Columbia, S.C. no date	fountain bowl
206.	Mr. and Mrs. Thomas H. Cooper 4 Orange Street Charleston, S.C. no date	garden plan
207.	Mr. and Mrs. Thomas H. Cooper 4 Orange Street Charleston, S.C. no date	garden plan
208.	Mr. and Mrs. Thomas H. Cooper 4 Orange Street Charleston, S.C. May 1974	sketch of gate
209.	Mr. and Mrs. Thomas H. Cooper 4 Orange Street Charleston, S.C. November 26, 1974	plan of gate
210.	Mr. and Mrs. Thomas H. Cooper 4 Orange Street Charleston, S.C. no date	garden plan
211.	R. H. Costigun White Plains, N.Y. no date	service screen and garden lattice
212.	Cotton Cabin Gipsy Trail Club Carmel, N.Y. no date	plan and elevation
213.	Mrs. R. E. Coulson Pelham Manor, N.Y. May 5, 1924	planting plan for flower garden
214.	Mr. and Mrs. Earl Craig Beaver, Pa. November 12, 1936	detail garden layout and brick construction plan

REF. NO.	ORIGINAL OWNER / LOCATION	AVAILABLE INFORMATION
215.	Mr. and Mrs. Earl Craig Beaver, Pa. November 9, 1936	utility location plan
216.	Earl Craig Beaver, Pa. November 15, 1940	winter screens and plants
217.	The Crescent Charleston, S.C. September 1926	colored general plan, Olmsted Brothers
218.	Crippled Children Center Calhoun Street Charleston, S.C. no date	proposed parking layout
219.	Crippled Children Center Calhoun Street Charleston, S.C. no date	proposed parking layout
220.	Crippled Children Center Calhoun Street Charleston, S.C. March 1966	plot plan
221.	Glen H. Curtis Memorial H.S. Hammondsport, N.Y. November 9, 1934	preliminary plan of grounds—rendered
222.	Mr. Carlton G. Davies 6 Lamboll Street Charleston, S.C. June 27, 1961	parking space and entrance drive
223.	Mr. and Mrs. Carlton Davies 175 Rutledge Avenue Charleston, S.C. February 23, 1950	garden plan
224.	A. P. Davin, Esq. New Castle, N.Y. March 31, 1939	plan of landscape arrangement
225.	C. Stuart Dawson, Esq. Charleston, S.C. February 28, 1949	garden design
226.	Mr. and Mrs. William B. Deas Charleston, S.C. January 22, 1958	landscape plan
227.	Mr. and Mrs. William B. Deas 72 Murray Boulevard Charleston, S.C. October 16, 1968	garden plan

REF. NO.	ORIGINAL OWNER / LOCATION	AVAILABLE INFORMATION
228.	Mr. and Mrs. William B. Deas 72 Murray Boulevard Charleston, S.C. October 16, 1968	garden plan
229.	Defense Housing Project Charleston, S.C. June 30, 1942	planting plan, SC 38061
230.	Defense Housing Project Federal Works Agency Charleston, S.C. March 4, 1941	planting plan, block 1, SC 38025
231.	Mr. and Mrs. Raymond M. Demere Harrington Hall Savannah, Ga. February 28, 1946	sketch of garden gate
232.	Mr. and Mrs. Raymond M. Demere Harrington Hall—Plantation Harbor Savannah, Ga. January 25, 1946	sketch plan landscape suggestions
233.	Gregory M. Dexter White Plains, N.Y. no date	planting plan
234.	J. N. Dodson, Esq. Pelham Manor, N.Y. September 5, 1929	construction plan of garden
235.	Dominion Hills Berkeley County, S.C. January 18, 1968	subdivision tract
236.	James P. Donahue, Esq. Southampton, N.Y. March 7, 1929	deck floor plan of plunge and glass passageway
237.	Dorchester County South Carolina 1939	general highways and transportation map
238.	R. A. Dorman, Esq. Bronxville, N.Y. July 29, 1924	construction plan of garden
239.	E. Gaillard Dotterer, Esq. 16 Atlantic Street Charleston, S.C. November 26, 1956	garden
240.	Nelson Doubleday, Esq. Bonny Hall Yemassee, S.C. no date	sketch for two garden gates

REF. NO.	ORIGINAL OWNER / LOCATION	AVAILABLE INFORMATION
241.	Nelson Doubleday, Esq. Bonny Hall Yemassee, S.C. May 1, 1935	additions and improvements
242.	Mr. and Mrs. Francis Dougherty 50 Legare Street Charleston, S.C. February 10, 1969	design of patio, drive, and gates
243.	Mr. and Mrs. Francis Dougherty 50 Legare Street Charleston, S.C. February 10, 1969	design of patio, drive, and gates
244.	Mr. and Mrs. Francis Dougherty 50 Legare Street Charleston, S.C. February 5, 1969	design of patio, drive, and gates
245.	Mr. and Mrs. Francis Dougherty 50 Legare Street Charleston, S.C. February 5, 1969	design of patio, drive, and gates
246.	Doylestown Emergency Hospital Doylestown, Pa. June 1, 1950	construction plan
247.	Doylestown Emergency Hospital Doylestown, Pa. November 9, 1949	preliminary plan of grounds
248.	Doylestown Emergency Hospital Doylestown, Pa. June 20, 1950	construction plan of grounds
249.	Doylestown Emergency Hospital Doylestown, Pa. June 1, 1950	construction plan of grounds
250.	Arthur L. Drew, Esq. Pleasantville, N.Y. no date	aerial perspective
251.	Frank L. Dunlap, Esq. Springfield, Mass. September 12, 1922	general plan
252.	O. W. Dunn, Esq. Pleasantville, N.Y. no date	plan of an old-fashioned garden
253.	Mr. and Mrs. Leon Rogers Drake, Jr. 122 Tradd Street Charleston, S.C. March 10, 1969	garden plan

REF. NO.	ORIGINAL OWNER / LOCATION	AVAILABLE INFORMATION
254.	Mr. and Mrs. Leon Rogers Drake, Jr. 122 Tradd Street Charleston, S.C. May 5, 1971	pool and fountain
255.	Mr. and Mrs. Leon Rogers Drake, Jr. 122 Tradd Street Charleston, S.C. May 5, 1971	pool and fountain
256.	Mr. and Mrs. George Easterbrook Hillsdale, N.Y. September 16, 1955	sketch plan of garage court and parking space
257.	Edisto Island South Carolina 1918	topography
258.	Mrs. Edward Ely Tradd Street Charleston, S.C. November 23, 1932	garden plan
259.	Mr. and Mrs. Stuart Elliott 165 Cherokee Road Charlotte, N.C. May 1970	general plan and garden
260.	Esso station Corner of Meeting and Chalmers Charleston, S.C. January 11, 1971	plan and specification for construction and planting
261.	Oscar Ettari, Esq. Bridge Valley November 4, 1946	terrace
262.	O. E. Ettari, Esq. New Rochelle, N.Y. no date	planting plan
263.	O. E. Ettari, Esq. New Rochelle, N.Y. May 4, 1926	perennial plan
264.	Exchange and Prioleau Streets no date	first-floor plan
265.	Fairview Memorial Park Fairview, N.J. April 29, 1935	parking plan
266.	Mr. and Mrs. Elliott Farr no location September 24, 1956	landscape plan
267.	Federal Works Agency Charleston, S.C. September 4, 1941	planting plan, block 3

REF. NO.	ORIGINAL OWNER / LOCATION	AVAILABLE INFORMATION
268.	Federal Works Agency Charleston, S.C. September 4, 1941	planting plan, block 3, SC 38025
269.	The Federated Garden Clubs of New York State October 30, 1936	International Flower Show, general construction plan for exhibit
270.	The Federated Garden Clubs of New York State October 30, 1936	details, sheet no. 2
271.	The Federated Garden Club of New York State 1937	International Flower Show, plan of exhibit
272.	The Federated Garden Club of New York State February 3, 1937	details of exhibit, sheet no. 3
273.	The Federated Garden Club of New York State July 9, 1936	sketches for exhibit
274.	The Federated Garden Club of New York State no date	sketch of exhibit elevation and plan
275.	Mr. and Mrs. Franco Ferreira Buckingham, Pa. September 25, 1946	garden
276.	First Federal Savings and Loan Chalmers Street Charleston, S.C. February 15, 1963	parking plan no. 1
277.	First Federal Savings and Loan Chalmers Street Charleston, S.C. January 3, 1963	preliminary plan, parking and entrance
278.	First Federal Savings and Loan Chalmers Street Charleston, S.C. January 30, 1963	rendered planting plan
279.	First Federal Savings and Loan Association Charleston, S.C. January 30, 1963	planting plan
280.	First Federal Savings and Loan Association Charleston, S.C. January 30, 1963	planting plan with field notes

REF. NO.	ORIGINAL OWNER / LOCATION	AVAILABLE INFORMATION
281.	First Federal Savings and Loan Association Chalmers and State Streets Charleston, S.C. February 20, 1969	parking lot
282.	First Federal Savings and Loan Association Charleston, S.C. January 14, 1963	construction plan, parking and entrance
283.	First Federal Savings and Loan Association Charleston, S.C. December 29, 1975	planting plan
284.	Fischer and Porter Co. Hatboro, Pa. October 18, 1951	plan of base grades, southeast section of site
285.	Ft. Moultrie Mt. Pleasant, S.C. 1918	topography
286.	Mr. and Mrs. G. C. Frampton 16 Orange Street Charleston, S.C. November 1947	garden plan
287.	Hon. J. S. Frelinghuysen Rice Hope August 22, 1932	detail of garden walls
288.	First National Bank of S.C. Charleston, S.C. December 13, 1967	revision of parking
289.	First National Bank of S.C. Charleston, S.C. November 20, 1967	parking lot
290.	First National Bank of S.C. Charleston, S.C. January 20, 1968	final plan for paving and walls of parking lot
291.	First National Bank of S.C. Charleston, S.C. January 20, 1968	final plan for paving and walls
292.	Mr. and Mrs. A. C. Flint The Crescent Charleston, S.C. December 2, 1963	general plan of grounds with field notes
293.	Mr. and Mrs. A. C. Flint The Crescent Charleston, S.C. January 18, 1964	construction plan—drive, parking, grading brick paving, fences, and gates

REF. NO.	ORIGINAL OWNER / LOCATION	AVAILABLE INFORMATION
294.	Mr. and Mrs. A. C. Flint The Crescent Charleston, S.C. January 23, 1964	planting plan
295.	Mr. and Mrs. A. C. Flint Charleston, S.C. June 22, 1960	foundation plan, first-floor plan, second-floor plan, elevations, wood details, porch construction
296.	Mr. and Mrs. A. C. Flint The Crescent Charleston, S.C. December 2, 1963	general plan of grounds
297.	Mr. and Mrs. A. C. Flint The Crescent Charleston, S.C. January 10, 1964	general plan of grounds
298.	Mr. and Mrs. A. C. Flint The Crescent Charleston, S.C. January 23, 1964	planting plan
299.	Mr. and Mrs. A. C. Flint The Crescent Charleston, S.C. January 18, 1964	construction plan—drive, parking, grading, brick paving, fences, and gates
300.	Mr. and Mrs. A. C. Flint The Crescent Charleston, S.C. December 2, 1963	general plan of grounds
301.	J. F. Floyd Memorial Park St. Andrews Parish Charleston, S.C. September 18, 1956	road plan and tower location
302.	J. F. Floyd Mortuary, Inc. Spartanburg, S.C. May 2, 1956	Charleston Cemetery
303.	Hon. J. S. Frelinghuysen Rice Hope August 26, 1932	details of garden walls
304.	Hon. J. S. Frelinghuysen Rice Hope August 26, 1932	wood details—entrance gate
305.	Hon. J. S. Frelinghuysen Rice Hope no date	entrance gate detail—post top
306.	Hon. J. S. Frelinghuysen Rice Hope no date	entrance gate detail—post bottom

REF. NO.	ORIGINAL OWNER / LOCATION	AVAILABLE INFORMATION
307.	Hon. J. S. Frelinghuysen Rice Hope Charleston, S.C. November 9, 1932	sketch of entrance gate
308.	Senator J. S. Frelinghuysen no date	arch and lattice detail
309.	Senator J. S. Frelinghuysen Raritan, N.J. no date	plan of grounds for refreshment stand
310.	Gadsden House E. Bay Charleston, S.C. November 22, 1959	plan of grounds
311.	Mr. and Mrs. F. W. Garnjost (2) Spuyten Duyvil, N.Y. October 18, 1922	sketch plan of landscape
312.	Mr. and Mrs. F. W. Garnjost (2) Spuyten Duyvil, N.Y. October 18, 1922	sketch plan of landscape
313.	Mr. and Mrs. F. W. Garnjost Spuyten Duyvil, N.Y. October 19, 1922	sketch of front elevation planting
314.	Mr. and Mrs. F. W. Garnjost Spuyten Duyvil, N.Y. February 20, 1923	planting plan
315.	F. W. Garnjost, Esq. Spuyten Duyvil, N.Y. June 4, 1923	perennial border
316.	General Electric Summerville, S.C. May 1, 1968	exterior elevations of details, office area, 7010-(A) 245
317.	General Electric Summerville, S.C. November 1969	planting plan no. 1
318.	General Electric Summerville, S.C. January 10, 1970	planting plan for guardhouse and parking lot
319.	General Electric Summerville, S.C. January 12, 1970	planting plan no. 1, 2, 3, 4
320.	General Electric Summerville, S.C. December 20, 1967	general grading plan, 7010-(C) 105
321.	General Electric Summerville, S.C. December 20, 1967	general grading plan with colored areas, 7010-(C) 105

REF. NO.	ORIGINAL OWNER / LOCATION	AVAILABLE INFORMATION
322.	General Electric Summerville, S.C. December 20, 1967	general grading plan with colored areas, 7010-(C) 106
323.	General Electric Summerville, S.C. December 20, 1967	general grading plan, clearing and grubbing plan, 7010-(C) 104
324.	General Electric Summerville, S.C. January 12, 1970	planting plan no. 4
325.	General Electric Summerville, S.C. January 12, 1970	planting plan no. 3
326.	General Electric Summerville, S.C. January 12, 1970	planting plan no. 2
327.	General Electric Summerville, S.C. January 12, 1970	planting plan no. 1
328.	General Electric Summerville, S.C. January 12, 1970	planting plan for guardhouse and parking lot
329.	General Electric Summerville, S.C. January 12, 1970	planting plan no. 4
330.	General Electric Summerville, S.C. January 12, 1970	planting plan no. 4
331.	General Electric Summerville, S.C. January 12, 1970	planting plan no. 1
332.	General Electric Summerville, S.C. January 10, 1970	planting plan for guardhouse and parking lot
333.	General Electric Summerville, S.C. Rev. January 30, 1970	planting plan for guardhouse and parking lot
334.	General Electric Summerville, S.C. January 30, 1970	planting plan no. 4
335.	General Electric Summerville, S.C. February 16, 1980	planting plan no. 3
336.	General Electric Summerville, S.C. February 16, 1980	planting plan no. 2

REF. NO.	ORIGINAL OWNER / LOCATION	AVAILABLE INFORMATION
337.	General Electric Summerville, S.C. February 16, 1980	planting plan no. 1
338.	Armory Georgetown, S.C. no date	sketch of gun mounts
339.	Library grounds Georgetown, S.C. May 20, 1953	plan of gardens
340.	Mr. and Mrs. Coming Ball Gibbs Meeting Street Charleston, S.C. November 23, 1964	garden plan
341.	Mr. Louis M. Gourdin No. 19 Church Street Charleston, S.C. January 6, 1940	garage
342.	Mr. and Mrs. Louis M. Gourdin No. 13 Church Street October 18, 1940	rendered garden paths and fountains
343.	Mr. and Mrs. Louis M. Gourdin No. 13 Church Street Charleston, S.C. October 18, 1940	garden paths and fountains
344.	Mr. and Mrs. Louis M. Gourdin No. 19 Church Street Charleston, S.C. October 23, 1940	garden paths and fountain
345.	Grace Church (3) Charleston, S.C. September 25, 1958	addition and parish house sheets no. 1, 3, and 7
346.	Grace Church Charleston, S.C. March 30, 1959	garden—preliminary
347.	Grace Church Charleston, S.C. December 16, 1960	sketch of the Garden of Remembrance
348.	Grace Church Charleston, S.C. March 30, 1959	garden—preliminary with field notes
349.	Grace Church Charleston, S.C. December 16, 1960	Garden of Remembrance—planting plan and construction details
350.	Grace Church Charleston, S.C. July 28, 1959	construction plan of garden

REF. NO.	ORIGINAL OWNER / LOCATION	AVAILABLE INFORMATION
351.	Grace Church Charleston, S.C. December 16, 1960	Garden of Remembrance planting plan and construction plan
352.	Mr. Wm. R. Gracey, Esq. New Rochelle, N.Y. no date	perennial garden
353.	Mr. Wm. R. Gracey, Esq. New Rochelle, N.Y. February 1, 1928	grading and construction plan
354.	Mrs. C. E. Graham East Orange, N.J. April 11, 1933	general construction plan
355.	Mrs. C. E. Graham East Orange, N.J. October 5, 1933	plan of garden
356.	Granit Bronze, Inc. January 23, 1967	modified design of planter
357.	Mr. and Mrs. L. Louis Green III 21 King Street Charleston, S.C. April 5, 1963	garden design
358.	Mr. and Mrs. L. Louis Green III No. 21 King Street Charleston, S.C. June 16, 1963	rendered garden design
359.	Greenlawn Memorial Gardens Spartanburg, S.C. November 21, 1961	mausoleum garden, sketch of plan no. 1
360.	Greenlawn Memorial Gardens Spartanburg, S.C. November 20, 1961	plan no. 1—mausoleum garden
361.	Greenlawn Memorial Gardens Spartanburg, S.C. November 24, 1961	sketch of plan no. 1 mausoleum garden
362.	Greenlawn Memorial Gardens Spartanburg, S.C. November 23, 1961	sketch plan no. 2, mausoleum garden
363.	Greenlawn Memorial Gardens Spartanburg, S.C. February 1, 1962	plan of mausoleum gardens
364.	Greenlawn Memorial Gardens Spartanburg, S.C. no date	studies of plot layouts

REF. NO.	ORIGINAL OWNER / LOCATION	AVAILABLE INFORMATION
365.	Dr. and Mrs. H. B. Gregorie 37 King Street Charleston, S.C. no date	home garden design
366.	Mrs. William S. Grey Greenwich, Conn. no date	sketch plan a boxwood garden at Greystone
367.	Mr. and Mrs. A. D. Griffith Orangeburg, S.C. December 1, 1951	general plan
368.	Mr. and Mrs. A. D. Griffith Orangeburg, S.C. February 18, 1952	construction plan
369.	Mr. Foster Gunnison 207 East 45 Street, N.Y. July 13, 1934	foundation planting
370.	Gunntown Road or S.R. 2371 no date	topography map
371.	Guy Street, Clark Street, and Linwood Street San Diego, Calif. no date	preliminary for design study only
372.	Mr. and Mrs. J. M. Hagood 16 Legare Street Charleston, S.C. September 8, 1947	plan of garden
373.	Mr. and Mrs. J. M. Hagood Cashiers, N.C. May 17, 1961	preliminary plan, drive, parking, grading, and drainage with field notes
374.	Mr. and Mrs. J. M. Hagood Cashiers, N.C. June 19, 1961	construction plan with field notes
375.	Mr. and Mrs. J. M. Hagood Cashiers, N.C. June 19, 1961	construction plan
376.	Mr. and Mrs. J. M. Hagood Cashiers, N.C. May 17, 1961	preliminary plan, drive, parking, grading, and drainage
377.	Mr. and Mrs. J. M. Hagood Pon-Top-It High Hampton, N.C. January 10, 1962	plan of planting
378.	Mr. and Mrs. James M. Hagood 23 Meeting Street Charleston, S.C. October 30, 1965	garden design

REF. NO.	ORIGINAL OWNER / LOCATION	AVAILABLE INFORMATION
379.	Mr. and Mrs. James M. Hagood 23 Meeting Street Charleston, S.C. January 20, 1970	construction plan of garden no. 1
380.	Mr. and Mrs. James M. Hagood 23 Meeting Street Charleston, S.C. February 2, 1970	construction plan of garden no. 2
381.	Mr. and Mrs. James M. Hagood 23 Meeting Street Charleston, S.C. April 21, 1970	construction plan no. 3, tool house and lattice
382.	Mr. and Mrs. James M. Hagood 23 Meeting Street Charleston, S.C. January 20, 1970	construction plan of garden no. 1
383.	Mr. and Mrs. James M. Hagood 23 Meeting Street Charleston, S.C. October 30, 1969	garden design
384.	Mr. and Mrs. James M. Hagood 23 Meeting Street Charleston, S.C. February 2, 1970	plan no. 2 for garden pool
385.	Mr. and Mrs. James M. Hagood 23 Meeting Street Charleston, S.C. February 5, 1970	site plan, electrical
386.	Mr. Gordon Langley Hall 56 Society Street Charleston, S.C. June 5, 1962	remodeling
387.	Gordon Langley Hall, Esq. 56 Society Street Charleston, S.C. September 10, 1962	construction plan of drive and patio
388.	Gordon Langley Hall, Esq. 56 Society Street Charleston, S.C. September 1, 1962	sketch of drive and patio
389.	Gordon Langley Hall, Esq. 56 Society Street Charleston, S.C. September 1, 1962	sketch of drive and patio

REF. NO.	ORIGINAL OWNER / LOCATION	AVAILABLE INFORMATION
390.	Gordon Langley Hall, Esq. 56 Society Street Charleston, S.C. May 10, 1962	general plan of grounds
391.	Mr. Roger Hallowell (see McCain) Montgomery Avenue Ft. Washington, Pa. July 23, 1948	sketch of flagstone terrace
392.	E. W. Hammons Mamaroneck, N.Y. no date	construction drawings of wall at entrance
393.	Dr. and Mrs. Richard W. Hanckel, Jr. 71 Church Street Charleston, S.C. no date	garden plan
394.	Dr. and Mrs. Richard W. Hanckel, Jr. 71 Church Street Charleston, S.C. February 11, 1949	garden plan
395.	Harmon Park Marion, S.C. December 6, 1946	landscape plan
396.	Harmon Park Marion, S.C. March 1943	map of park and lots
397.	Mr. and Mrs. Anthony Harrigan 54 Legare Street Charleston, S.C. February 11, 1969	landscape plan
398.	Dr. S. M. Hart Port Chester, N.Y. no date	planting plan
399.	37 Hasell Street Charleston, S.C. no date	plan of old garden
400.	Mr. and Mrs. John H. Hathaway Church Lane and Hathaway Road Berkely Section, Scarsdale, N.Y. June 15, 1939	elevations, cellar plan, first-floor plan, second-floor plan
401.	Mr. and Mrs. M. D. Haven 13 East Bay Street Charleston, S.C. February 14, 1949	garden design
402.	Mr. and Mrs. M. D. Haven 13 East Bay Street Charleston, S.C. March 22, 1949	garden design

REF. NO.	ORIGINAL OWNER / LOCATION	AVAILABLE INFORMATION
403.	Mr. and Mrs. M. D. Haven Charleston, S.C. September 17, 1949	construction drawings of arch and mirror frame
404.	Dr. and Mrs. John C. Hawk, Jr. 1 Meeting Street Charleston, S.C. October 27, 1967	planting plan
405.	Mrs. Rees Hawkins Charleston, S.C. March 26, 1929	full-size section of pool
406.	W. T. P. Hazard, Esq. Brookville, L.I. August 12, 1930	sketch plan of grounds
407.	Mr. Carl H. Heineman Ridley Park, Pa. July 2, 1919	sketch of subdivision and arrangement of lots
408.	Mr. and Mrs. Louis L. Henninger, Jr. Johnson Road The Crescent Charleston, S.C. February 17, 1955	landscape plan no. 1
409.	Mrs. William L. Hewitt February 2, 1956	sketch for screen planting
410.	Mrs. William L. Hewitt February 2, 1956	sketch for screen planting
411.	Mr. and Mrs. E. M. Hickey (see Kite) Seabrook Island, S.C. February 11, 1974	site plan
412.	Mr. and Mrs. E. M. Hickey (see Kite) Seabrook Island, S.C. December 30, 1974	landscape plan
413.	Mr. and Mrs. E. M. Hickey (See Kite) Seabrook Island, S.C. December 30, 1974	landscape plan
414.	Highland Grade School White Plains, N.Y. no date	general plan of grounds
415.	Highlands Grade School White Plains, N.Y. no date	sketch of planting in relation to elevation of building
416.	Highland Memorial Cemetery Knoxville, Tennessee September 9, 1955	Masonic Gardens
417.	Miss Margaretta S. Hinchman Gladwyne, Pa. January 22, 1951	house location and contours plan

REF. NO.	ORIGINAL OWNER / LOCATION	AVAILABLE INFORMATION
418.	Miss Margaretta S. Hinchman Gladwyne, Pa. January 22, 1951	elevations, electrical
419.	Miss Margaretta S. Hinchman Gladwyne, Pa. January 22, 1951	plans
420.	Hispanic Building Corp. Larchmont, N.Y.	pool detail, Chatsworth Gardens
421.	Hispanic Building Corp. Chatsworth and Murray Ave. Larchmont, N.Y. April 22, 1928	detail of curving steps, apt. garden
422.	Historic Charleston Foundation 40, 42, and 43 Society Street 64, 66 and 72 Anson St. Charleston, S.C. June 24, 1960	site plan
423.	Historic Charleston Foundation 328 East Bay Street Charleston, S.C. September 20, 1963	concrete steps and plans for grounds
424.	Historic Charleston Foundation 63 Laurens St. and 74 Anson St. Charleston, S.C. December 2, 1966	construction plan for gates, fences, walks, patio, and steps
425.	John Hoar, Esq. Hunridge Farm Epping, N.H. September 23, 1940	plan for early America dooryard
426.	Mr. and Mrs. Donald Hobart Meeting St. Charleston, S.C. October 1959	plan of garden and grounds with construction details
427.	Mr. and Mrs. Donald Hobart Meeting St. Charleston, S.C. October 1959	plan of garden and grounds with construction details
428.	Mrs. Duncan Homes Brookville, L.I., N.Y. September 29, 1932	plan of garden alterations
429.	Mrs. William I. Holt Charleston, S.C. December 16, 1959	construction plan of terrace garden
430.	Mr. and Mrs. J. T. Hopkins 70 King Street Charleston, S.C. January 14, 1955	landscape plan

REF. NO.	ORIGINAL OWNER / LOCATION	AVAILABLE INFORMATION
431.	Mr. and Mrs. Trenholm Hopkins 39 East Battery Charleston, S.C. May 18, 1958	elevation and floor plan
432.	Mr. and Mrs. J. Trenholm Hopkins 39 East Battery Charleston, S.C. May 18, 1958	floor plan and specifications
433.	Mr. and Mrs. Albert F. Howard Yeamans Hall, S.C. May 2, 1967	garden wall
434.	Mr. and Mrs. Albert F. Howard Yeamans Hall, S.C. May 2, 1967	garden wall
435.	Mr. and Mrs. Albert F. Howard Yeamans Hall, S.C. May 2, 1967	garden wall
436.	Mr. and Mrs. Albert F. Howard Yeamans Hall, S.C. October 15, 1966	construction and planting plan, garden
437.	Mr. and Mrs. Albert F. Howard Yeamans Hall, S.C. October 15, 1966	construction and planting plan, garden
438.	Mr. Daniel E. Huger 34 Meeting St. Charleston, S.C. February 1, 1959	court for three-car garage
439.	Mr. Daniel E. Huger 34 Meeting St. Charleston, S.C. February 1, 1959	court for three-car garage
440.	Mr. and Mrs. Daniel E. Huger 34 Meeting St. Charleston, S.C. November 24, 1959	plan of garden
441.	H. F. Hughes, Esq. Shoreham, L.I. January 8, 1923	perennial garden
442.	H. F. Hughes, Esq. Shoreham, L.I. January 6, 1923	general plan
443.	Hutchinson School Property North Pelham, N.Y. March 20, 1931	planting—grading and construction plan

REF. NO.	ORIGINAL OWNER / LOCATION	AVAILABLE INFORMATION
444.	Hutchinson School Property North Pelham, N.Y. June 16, 1932	grading and construction plan
445.	Mr. and Mrs. Thomas Huguenin Halidon Hill September 16, 1966	landscape recommendations
446.	Mr. and Mrs. Richard W. Hutson Charleston, S.C. July 1, 1960	plan of grounds
447.	Mr. and Mrs. J. Addison Ingle, Jr. 63 Meeting St. Charleston, S.C. no date	landscape plan
448.	Mr. and Mrs. J. Addison Ingle, Jr. 63 Meeting St. Charleston, S.C. no date	landscape plan
449.	Mr. and Mrs. J. Addison Ingle, Jr. 63 Meeting Street Charleston, S.C. no date	pencil sketch of site plan
450.	International Longshoremen Assoc. S. Market and E. Bay Charleston, S.C. February 2, 1970	site plan
451.	International Longshoremen Assoc. S. Market and E. Bay Charleston, S.C.	site plan with field notes
452.	International Longshoremen Assoc. S. Market and E. Bay Charleston, S.C. February 17, 1970	site plan—walls, fence, and planting
453.	International Longshoremen Assoc. 471 E. Bay Street Charleston, S.C. February 3, 1967	construction plan and planting indication
454.	International Longshoremen Assoc. 471 E. Bay Street Charleston, S.C. February 3, 1967	construction plan and planting indication
455.	International Longshoremen Assoc. 471 E. Bay Street Charleston, S.C. February 17, 1970	site plan—wall, fence, planting for addition to parking area

REF. NO.	ORIGINAL OWNER / LOCATION	AVAILABLE INFORMATION
456.	International Longshoremen Assoc. E. Bay Street Charleston, S.C. November 1967	planting plan
457.	Mr. Oliver Iselin, Sr. Scottswood Plantation, S.C. February 25, 1957	planting plan for school
458.	Mr. Oliver Iselin, Sr. Scottswood Plantation February 25, 1957	planting plan for school
459.	G. S. Jacobson, Esq. New Rochelle, N.Y. January 29, 1925	planting plan
460.	James Island Quadrangle James Island, S.C. surveyed 1918	topography—Dept. of Interior
461.	Dr. and Mrs. Pierre G. Jenkins Riverland Terrace June 7, 1960	plan of terrace
462.	Mr. and Mrs. R.H. Jennings Orangeburg, S.C. December 20, 1949	garden design
463.	Bascom Johnson, Esq. Pleasantville, N.Y. no date	perennial garden
464.	J. W. Johnson Spuyten Duyvil, N.Y. no date	handrail detail
465.	J. W. Johnson, Esq. Spuyten Duyvil, N.Y. October 19, 1926	construction plan for grounds
466.	J. W. Johnson Spuyten Duyvil, N.Y. no date	wrought-iron stair rail
467.	J. W. Johnson, Esq. Spuyten Duyvil, N.Y. November 11, 1926	detail of steps
468.	S. Lewis Johnson, Esq. No. 16–20 Lamboll St. Charleston, S.C. March 21, 1949	sketch plan no. 2 garden and grounds
469.	Dr. Rufus P. Johnston Briarcliff, N.Y. December 27, 1922	general plan

REF. NO.	ORIGINAL OWNER / LOCATION	AVAILABLE INFORMATION
470.	Mr. and Mrs. C. S. Jones Summerville, S.C. April 5, 1948	garden plan
471.	Mr. and Mrs. Cadwallader Jones The Crescent Charleston, S.C. February 20, 1958	landscape design
472.	Mr. and Mrs. C. S. Jones Summerville, S.C. February 25, 1948	colonial garden gate and fence, garden detail
473.	Mr. Richard Kaminski Georgetown, S.C. February 5, 1953	house location and general plan of grounds
474.	Mr. Richard Kaminski Georgetown, S.C. February 5, 1953	house location and general plan of grounds
475.	Mr. and Mrs. Nathan Kaminski Georgetown, S.C. April 5, 1965	garden plan and details of terrace, wall, and pool
476.	Mr. and Mrs. Nathan Kaminski Georgetown, S.C. April 5, 1965	garden plan and details of terrace, wall, and pool
477.	Mr. Joseph Kerrigan Oyster Bay, L.I. no date	sketch plan of garden
478.	Mr. Joseph Kerrigan Oyster Bay, L.I. no date	preliminary sketch elevation of garden terraces
479.	Mrs. William B. King 53A South Battery Charleston, S.C. April 4, 1972	plan of garden
480.	Mrs. William B. King 53A South Battery Charleston, S.C. April 4, 1972	plan of garden
481.	Mrs. William B. King 53A South Battery Charleston, S.C. April 4, 1972	plan of garden
482.	Mrs. G. Kirkwood King Meeting St. Charleston, S.C. April 8, 1958	sketch plan of planting

REF. NO.	ORIGINAL OWNER / LOCATION	AVAILABLE INFORMATION
483.	68 King St. Charleston, S.C. no date	site layout plan
484.	Mr. and Mrs. I. M. Kite (see Hickey) Seabrook Island, S.C. February 11, 1974	site plan
485.	Mr. and Mrs. Avram Kronsberg 44 Society St. Charleston, S.C. February 27, 1964	planting plan
486.	Mr. and Mrs. Avram Kronsberg 44 Society Street Charleston, S.C. April 16, 1963	construction plan, garden and drive
487.	Mr. and Mrs. Avram Kronsberg 44 Society Street Charleston, S.C. March 18, 1963	general plan
488.	Mr. and Mrs. Avram Kronsberg 44 Society Street Charleston, S.C. June 6, 1963	garden tool house
489.	Mr. and Mrs. Avram Kronsberg 44 Society Street Charleston, S.C. June 6, 1963	garden tool house
490.	Mr. and Mrs. Avram Kronsberg 44 Society Street Charleston, S.C. April 16, 1963	construction plan, garden and drive
491.	Davis Laing, Esq. Pelham Manor, N.Y. July 31, 1929	construction plan of garden
492.	Davis Laing, Esq. Pelham Manor, N.Y. August 19, 1929	lattice screen detail
493.	Lake Park City of Charleston Calhoun Street and Lockwood Drive Charleston, S.C. February 10, 1964	planting plan
494.	Lake Park City of Charleston Calhoun Street and Lockwood Drive Charleston, S.C. February 10, 1964	planting plan

REF. NO.	ORIGINAL OWNER / LOCATION	AVAILABLE INFORMATION
495.	Mr. Frank E. Lapham, Jr. Summit Avenue Hackensack, N.J. August 29, 1927	fence elevation
496.	Mr. Frank E. Lapham, Jr. Summit Avenue Hackensack, N.J. July 22, 1927	sketch plan
497.	Mr. and Mrs. L. H. Laughlin Winant Road Princeton, N.J. May 15, 1957	construction plan, walls, walks, terrace, and pool
498.	Mr. and Mrs. Edgar H. Lawton Hartsville, S.C. December 4, 1940	general plan of landscape development
499.	Mr. and Mrs. Edgar H. Lawton Hartsville, S.C. January 14, 1941	garden construction
500.	32 Legare Street Charleston, S.C. no date	plan of old garden
501.	Legareville Charleston County, S.C. 1918	topography
502.	Charles R. Leonard, Esq. (3) Jericho, L.I. May 25, 1927	house elevations
503.	Mrs. Alicia Legg Hackensack, N.J. October 1, 1929	f.s. details and roof final
504.	Mrs. Alicia Legg Hackensack, N.J. October 1, 1929	garden house
505.	Mrs. Alicia Legg Hackensack, N.J. October 1, 1929	garden house
506.	Mrs. Alicia Legg Hackensack, N.J. October 1, 1929	f.s. details and roof final
507.	Mrs. Alicia Legg (2) Hackensack, N.J. October 1, 1929	f.s. details and section "b-b"
508.	Ms. Alicia Legg no date	rose arbor

REF. NO.	ORIGINAL OWNER / LOCATION	AVAILABLE INFORMATION
509.	Mrs. Charles R. Leonard Jericho, L.I., N.Y. October 12, 1931	flower border
510.	Mrs. Charles R. Leonard Jericho, L.I., N.Y. May 14, 1929	general plan—south of house
511.	Mrs. Charles R. Leonard Jericho, L.I., N.Y. no date	sketch of proposed new drive
512.	Mrs. Charles R. Leonard Jericho, L.I., N.Y. no date	flower border for cutting
513.	Mrs. Charles R. Leonard Jericho, L.I., N.Y. September 23, 1932	terrace—steps and pool
514.	Mrs. Charles R. Leonard Jericho, L.I., N.Y. May 11, 1928	plan no. 1 of paved area
515.	Leonard Estates Long Island no date	road centerline elevations
516.	Mrs. Charles R. Leonard Jericho, L.I. no date	sketch of gate
517.	Mrs. Charles Leonard Jericho, L.I., N.Y. February 15, 1929	sketch no. 2—gate and fence
518.	Leonard no location no date	diagram showing approximate location of trees
519.	Mr. and Mrs. Richard C. Lewis 8 Bedon's Alley Charleston, S.C. January 22, 1957	terrace garden
520.	Dr. and Mrs. I. Grier Linton no location November 27, 1964	garden plan and details of pool
521.	Litchfield, Conn. July 30, 1956	church by Henry P. Staats, architect— elevations and plans
522.	Live Oak Memorial Garden Charleston, S.C. December 18, 1956	Garden of Religion with field notes
523.	Live Oak Memorial Gardens Charleston, S.C. December 11, 1956	drive and tower locations with grading plan

REF. NO.	ORIGINAL OWNER / LOCATION	AVAILABLE INFORMATION
524.	Live Oak Memorial Gardens Charleston, S.C. no date	Garden of Four Apostles
525.	Live Oak Memorial Gardens Charleston, S.C. June 28, 1960	general plan no. 2
526.	Live Oak Memorial Gardens Charleston, S.C. May 27, 1957	Garden of Religion
527.	Live Oak Memorial Gardens St. Andrews Parish Charleston, S.C. May 2, 1956	preliminary sketch no. 3
528.	Live Oak Memorial Gardens St. Andrews Parish Charleston, S.C. June 27, 1957	general plan
529.	Live Oak Memorial Gardens Charleston, S.C. November 25, 1957	Garden of the Madonna and Child—plats
530.	Live Oak Memorial Gardens Charleston, S.C. October 28, 1957	Masonic Garden—plats
531.	Live Oak Memorial Gardens Charleston, S.C. March 12, 1957	immediate need area
532.	Live Oak Memorial Gardens Charleston, S.C. no date	plat
533.	Live Oak Memorial Gardens Charleston, S.C. October 3, 1956	Garden of Religion
534.	Live Oak Memorial Gardens Charleston, S.C. November 16, 1956	Garden of Religion with field notes
535.	Live Oak Memorial Gardens Charleston, S.C. June 27, 1957	general plan—part of Live Oak Memorial Gardens with field notes
536.	Garden of Religion Live Oak Memorial Gardens Charleston, S.C. May 27 1957	plan of planting and paving
538.	Live Oak Memorial Gardens Charleston, S.C. January 18, 1958	Garden of the Tower

REF. NO.	ORIGINAL OWNER / LOCATION	AVAILABLE INFORMATION
537.	Live Oak Memorial Gardens Charleston, S.C. November 20. 1957	planting plan for Live Oak
539.	Live Oak Memorial Gardens Charleston, S.C. January 18, 1958	rendered
540.	Live Oak Memorial Gardens Charleston, S.C. January 18, 1958	Garden at the Tower with field notes
541.	Live Oak Memorial Gardens Charleston, S.C. February 14, 1958	design of planting at gate
542.	Live Oak Memorial Gardens Charleston, S.C. February 14, 1958	planting at gate
543.	Live Oak Memorial Gardens Charleston, S.C. March 31, 1958	plan of service area
544.	Live Oak Memorial Gardens Charleston, S.C. April 22, 1958	details of marble for gateposts
545.	Live Oak Memorial Gardens Charleston, S.C. June 28, 1960	general plan no. 2
546.	Live Oak Memorial Gardens Charleston, S.C.	Masonic Garden
547.	Garden of the Four Apostles Live Oak Memorial Gardens Charleston, S.C. May 8, 1966	resurvey—grading and drainage
548.	Live Oak Memorial Gardens Charleston, S.C. May 8, 1966	plan—resurvey—grading and drainage, Garden of the Four Apostles
549.	Garden of Four Apostles Live Oak Memorial Gardens Charleston, S.C. May 8, 1966	resurvey—grading and drainage
550.	Live Oak Memorial Gardens Charleston, S.C. February 6, 1967	sketch of flag memorial setting
551.	Garden of the Four Apostles Live Oak Memorial Gardens Charleston, S.C. no date	plan of plats

REF. NO.	ORIGINAL OWNER / LOCATION	AVAILABLE INFORMATION
552.	Livingston and Haven, Inc. Charleston, S.C. April 21, 1965	plan—parking and planting
553.	13 Lowndes St. Charleston, S.C. April 4, 1956	construction plan of garden
554.	13 Lowndes St. Charleston, S.C. March 13, 1957	planting and construction plan of garden
555.	13 Lowndes St. Charleston, S.C. March 13, 1957	planting and construction plan of garden
556.	13 Lowndes St. Charleston, S.C. March 13, 1957	planting and construction plan of garden
557.	13 Lowndes St. no date	site plan of garden
558.	W. A. Lownds, Esq. Milburne, N.J. no date	perennial garden
559.	W. A. Lownds, Esq. Milburne, N.J. March 3, 1926	sketch plan for the property
560.	Lownds no location no date	site plan
561.	Luce Mepkin, S.C. no date	headstones
562.	Mr. Henry R. Luce Mepkin, S.C. September 16, 1946	sketch of gate
563.	Mr. Henry R. Luce Mepkin, S.C. August 21, 1937	main entrance gates
564.	Mr. and Mrs. Henry R. Luce Mepkin Plantation, S.C. November 17, 1937	plan of walks
565.	Mr. and Mrs. Henry R. Luce Mepkin Plantation, S.C. no date	plan of terrace—untitled
566.	Mr. and Mrs. Henry R. Luce Mepkin Plantation, S.C. 1937	plan of grading and soil preparation for camellia garden

REF. NO.	ORIGINAL OWNER / LOCATION	AVAILABLE INFORMATION
567.	Mr. and Mrs. Henry R. Luce Mepkin, S.C. no date	construction plan of camellia garden
568.	Mr. and Mrs. Henry R. Luce Mepkin, S.C. April 4, 1938	details of steps, walls, curbs, drainage and grading, garden
569.	Mr. and Mrs. Henry R. Luce Mepkin, S.C. no date	plan of planting for guesthouse group
570.	Mr. and Mrs. Henry R. Luce Mepkin, S.C. no date	details of garden gate
571.	Mr. and Mrs. Henry R. Luce Mepkin, S.C. February 12, 1944	enlargement of marker at Strawberry Chapel
572.	Section in Magnolia Cemetery Hartsville, S.C. December 11, 1945	landscape design
573.	Section in Magnolia Cemetery Hartsville, S.C. September 24, 1945	preliminary landscape design
574.	Magnolia Cemetery—plots 3, 6, 9 Hartsville, S.C. January 31, 1946	construction plan
575.	Plots 3, 6, 9 Magnolia Cemetery Hartsville, S.C. February 12, 1946	planting plan
576.	Magnolia Gardens Charleston, S.C. no date	map
577.	The Manor Club Pelham, N.Y. July 7, 1925	general plan
578.	Marine Corps Parris Island, S.C. no date	exchange complex
579.	Miss Grace Marks Riverside, Conn. April 7, 1930	rose garden lattice and gate
580.	Miss Grace Marks Riverside, Conn. no date	pool detail for garden

REF. NO.	ORIGINAL OWNER / LOCATION	AVAILABLE INFORMATION
581.	Mr. and Mrs. David L. Maybank, Jr. 8 Meeting St. Charleston, S.C. January 15, 1962	construction plan of garden
582.	Mr. and Mrs. David L. Maybank, Jr. 8 Meeting St. Charleston, S.C. November 30, 1962	planting plan of garden
583.	David L. Maybank Trident Industrial Park N. Charleston, S.C. February 17, 1975	Montgomery Ward warehouse and repair service facility
584.	David L. Maybank Trident Industrial Park N. Charleston, S.C. July 15, 1975	commercial bonded warehouse
585.	David L. Maybank Montgomery Ward Warehouse N. Charleston, S.C. May 6, 1976	drains and planting plan no. 2
586.	David L. Maybank Commercial Bonded Warehouse N. Charleston, S.C. April 16, 1976	drains and planting plan no. 1
587.	David L. Maybank Commercial Bonded Warehouse and Montgomery Ward Warehouse Trident Industrial Park N. Rhett Ave. N. Charleston, S.C. no date	irrigation system design—2
588.	Mr. and Mrs. David Maybank, Jr. 8 Meeting St. Charleston, S.C. no date	sketch of garden design
589.	Mr. and Mrs. David Maybank, Jr. 8 Meeting St. Charleston, S.C. no date	garden design
590.	David Maybank Commercial Bonded Warehouse Trident Industrial Park N. Rhett Ave. N. Charleston, S.C. no date	sprinkler design

REF. NO.	ORIGINAL OWNER / LOCATION	AVAILABLE INFORMATION
591.	David Maybank Montgomery Ward Warehouse Trident Industrial Park N. Rhett Ave. N. Charleston, S.C. no date	sprinkler design
592.	David Maybank Montgomery Ward Warehouse Trident Industrial Park N. Rhett Ave. N. Charleston, S.C. no date	sprinkler design
593.	Mrs. John Maybank 23 E. Bay Charleston, S.C. May 14, 1924	details of pool
	Mrs. John Maybank 23 E. Bay Charleston, S.C. February 28, 1972	garden plan no. 2
594.	Mrs. Joseph Maybank, Jr. 25 Meeting St. Charleston, S.C. May 27, 1941	sketch plan of garden
595.	Miss Hulda Witte Mazyck Legare St. Charleston, S.C. February 2, 1961	plan of grounds
596.	Miss Hulda Witte Mazyck Legare St. Charleston, S.C. February 2, 1961	plan of grounds
597.	Miss Elizabeth McCain 103 E. Court St. July 23, 1948	landscape plan
598.	Dr. and Mrs. R. J. McCradle Woodleigh Rd. Columbia, S.C. June 6, 1972	plot plan and building location, general landscape plan
599.	Dr. and Mrs. R. J. McCradle Woodleigh Rd. Columbia, S.C. May 24, 1972	plot plan and building location
600.	Dr. and Mrs. R. J. McCradle Woodleigh Rd. Columbia, S.C. May 24, 1972	preliminary general landscape plan

REF. NO.	ORIGINAL OWNER / LOCATION	AVAILABLE INFORMATION
601.	Dr. and Mrs. R. J. McCradle Columbia, S.C. May 1, 1973	construction plan—drive at entrance and rose garden
602.	Dr. and Mrs. R. J. McCradle Columbia, S.C. November 7, 1973	irrigation and planting plan
603.	Dr. and Mrs. R. J. McCradle Woodleigh Rd. Columbia, S.C. May 11, 1973	revised general landscape plan and construction details
604.	Dr. and Mrs. R. J. McCradle Woodleigh Rd. Columbia, S.C. January 10, 1974	plan—drive location and profile
605.	Mr. and Mrs. Frank McLeod, Jr. Winn St. Sumter, S.C. November 2, 1957	file no. 3380, sketch plan of property
606.	Mr. and Mrs. Frank McLeod, Jr. Winn St. Sumter, S.C. December 10, 1957	landscape plan
607.	Mepkin Plantation, S.C. no date	profile for steps
608.	Mepkin Plantation, S.C. no date	sketch
609.	Mr. and Mrs. Blake Middleton 42 Society St. Charleston, S.C. June 2, 1961	garden plan
610.	Mr. and Mrs. Blake Middleton 42 Society St. Charleston, S.C. June 2, 1961	garden plan and construction drawing
611.	Mr. and Mrs. Blake Middleton 42 Society St. Charleston, S.C. June 28, 1961	planting and construction drawing for garden
612.	Mr. William Middleton 83 Tradd St. Charleston, S.C. February 24, 1971	construction details—walls and paving
613.	Dr. and Mrs. William Middleton, Jr. 12 Meeting St. Charleston, S.C. March 25, 1971	entrance drive and gate

REF. NO.	ORIGINAL OWNER / LOCATION	AVAILABLE INFORMATION
614.	Mikell House 40 A-B-C Montagu St. Charleston, S.C. February 11, 1964	entrance drive
615.	Mikell House 40 A-B-C Montagu St. Charleston, S.C. March 3, 1964	entrance drive
616.	Mills-Hyatt House (2) Charleston, S.C. no date	garden plan and south wall with fountain
617.	Mills-Hyatt House Charleston, S.C. no date	study for electrical drawing in courtyard
618.	Mills-Hyatt House Charleston, S.C. April 21, 1969	study for plumbing in courtyard
619.	Mills-Hyatt House Charleston, S.C. September 2, 1970	construction plan—LA 1
620.	Mills-Hyatt House Charleston, S.C. July 29, 1970	construction plan—LA 3
621.	Mills-Hyatt House Charleston, S.C. May 11, 1970	general plan of patio and approach from Meeting Street
622.	Mills-Hyatt House Meeting St. Charleston, S.C.	seven guest floor plan
623.	Mills-Hyatt House Meeting St. Charleston, S.C. April 2, 1969	patio garden
624.	Mills-Hyatt House Meeting St. Charleston, S.C. August 3, 1970	construction plan LA 4—patio
625.	Mills-Hyatt House Meeting St. Charleston, S.C. October 1, 1970	paving detail LA 6—patio
626.	Mills-Hyatt House (2) Charleston, S.C. August 25, 1970	full-size capital

REF. NO.	ORIGINAL OWNER / LOCATION	AVAILABLE INFORMATION
627.	Mills-Hyatt House Charleston, S.C. July 16, 1970	plan of pool
628.	Mills-Hyatt House Charleston, S.C. May 12, 1969	general plan of patio and approach from Meeting Street with field notes
629.	Mills-Hyatt House Charleston, S.C. July 11, 1970	"rendered" general plan of patio and approach from Meeting Street
630.	Mills-Hyatt House Charleston, S.C. July 29, 1970	render construction plan LA 3
631.	Mills-Hyatt House Meeting Street Charleston, S.C. August 25, 1970	construction plan LA 3, patio—with flower paver in color
632.	Mills-Hyatt House Charleston, S.C. September 20, 1970	details of planter
633.	Mills-Hyatt House Meeting Street Charleston, S.C. September 21, 1970	trellis and gate—patio LA 5
634.	Mills-Hyatt House Charleston, S.C. July 24 1970	construction plan no. 2—patio
635.	Mills-Hyatt House Charleston, S.C. June 15, 1970	construction plan LA no. 1
636.	Mills-Hyatt House Charleston, S.C. October 3, 1970	planting plan LA 7
637.	Mills-Hyatt House Meeting Street Charleston, S.C. no date	courtyard
638.	Mills-Hyatt House Charleston, S.C. no date	garden plan and south wall
639.	Montagu and Rutledge Avenues Charleston, S.C. no date	proposed brick fence and iron gate, Montagu Street elevation
640.	Mrs. William G. Moore (see Hewitt and West) February 2, 1956	removal plan

REF. NO.	ORIGINAL OWNER / LOCATION	AVAILABLE INFORMATION
641.	Mrs. William G. Moore (see Hewitt and West) no date	plan and elevation—garden entrance
642.	Mrs. Victor Morawetz 30 Meeting Street Charleston, S.C. December 22, 1948	landscape design
643.	Mrs. Shirley W. Morgan Princeton, N.J. May 15, 1957	sketch plan—additions to garden
644.	Temple Israel Section Mount Pleasant Cemetery Westchester Co., N.Y. October 7, 1924	plan
645.	Mr. and Mrs. G. E. Muckenfuss Summerville, S.C. January 15, 1958	landscape design
646.	Mulberry Oakley, S.C. June 1930	landscape plan
647.	Mulberry Oakley, S.C. June 1930	landscape plan
648.	Mulberry Oakley, S.C. no date	garden gate
649.	Mulberry Oakley, S.C. June 16, 1930	garden walk gate
650.	Mulberry Oakley, S.C. June 18, 1930	garden gate
651.	Mulberry Oakley, S.C. January 18, 1937	details for gate on river walk
652.	Mulberry Oakley, S.C. June 30, 1930	detail of wall north end of house
653.	Mulberry Oakley, S.C. September 4, 1930	full-size detail for garden gate hinges
654.	Mulberry Oakley, S.C. September 21, 1930	full-size detail—gate straps and tops

REF. NO.	ORIGINAL OWNER / LOCATION	AVAILABLE INFORMATION
655.	Mulberry Oakley, S.C. no date	pool and bird fountain
656.	Mulberry Oakley, S.C. no date	wood details for garden gate
657.	12 Newin Rd. no location no date	planting plan
658.	Oakland Club (2) Near Pineville, S.C. February 12, 1937	gateway
659.	Mrs. Elizabeth R. Oughton Doylestown, Pa. August 9, 1947	construction plan, garden steps, walls, and drain
660.	Mr. and Mrs. F.D. Owen, Jr. Columbia, S.C. May 19, 1973	general landscape recommendations
661.	Palmer College 125 Bull Street Charleston, S.C. November 24, 1958	plan for grounds with field notes
662.	Palmer College 125 Bull Street Charleston, S.C. November 24, 1958	plan for grounds
663.	Park Hill White Birch Terrace and Park Lane Essex Falls and Caldwell, N.J. May 13, 1926	profile from Roseland Ave. to White Birch Terrace
664.	Dr. Edward F. Parker 160 Rutledge Avenue Charleston S.C. March 30, 1956	location plan for proposed buildings
665.	Dr. Edward F. Parker 160 Rutledge Avenue Charleston, S.C. April 18, 1956	three location plans for proposed buildings
666.	Mrs. Junius Parker Port Chester, N.Y. no date	sketch of garden
667.	Mrs. Edwin Parsons East Bay Street Charleston, S.C. November 21, 1941	planting plan

REF. NO.	ORIGINAL OWNER / LOCATION	AVAILABLE INFORMATION
668.	James C. Patterson, Esq. Bronxville, N.Y. September 1922	planting plan
669.	James C. Patterson, Esq. Bronxville, N.Y. July 24, 1922	garden plan
670.	Mr. and Mrs. Charles Paul III Wadmalaw Island, S.C. April 1, 1949	garden design
671.	Mrs. Charles Paul III 75 King Street Charleston, S.C. April 6, 1951	garden plan
672.	Mr. and Mrs. Charles Paul III 75 King Street Charleston, S.C. June 5, 1961	garden plan
673.	Mr. and Mrs. Charles Paul III 75 King St. Charleston, S.C. no date	garden plan
674.	R. E. Paul, Esq. Pleasantville, N.Y. no date	sketch plan of woods garden
675.	Pennstone Doylestown, Pa. October 18, 1945	revised plan
676.	Pennstone Doylestown, Pa. no date	location and construction plan of roads, walk, ret. walls, drain, and utility trench
677.	Pennstone Doylestown, Pa. September 14, 1954	plan of alterations
678.	Pennstone—on Turk Road Doylestown Pa. April 28, 1941	plans
679.	Pennstone—on Turk Road Doylestown, Pa. April 28, 1941	sections and elevations
680.	Mr. and Mrs. J. W. Pickens Orangeburg, S.C. October 12, 1950	planting plan
681.	Mr. and Mrs. J. W. Pickens Orangeburg, S.C. May 19, 1950	general landscape plan

REF. NO.	ORIGINAL OWNER / LOCATION	AVAILABLE INFORMATION
682.	Mr. and Mrs. J. W. Pickens, Jr. Moore Road Orangeburg, S.C. April 21, 1968	plan for house location and drive
683.	Mr. and Mrs. J. W. Pickens, Jr. Moore Road Orangeburg, S.C. February 17, 1969	plan of drive and entrance posts
684.	Mr. and Mrs. J. W. Pickens, Jr. Moore Road Orangeburg, S.C. February 17, 1969	plan of drive and entrance posts
685.	Mr. and Mrs. J. W. Pickens, Jr. Moore Road Orangeburg, S.C. April 21, 1968	plan of house location and drive
686.	Mr. and Mrs. J. W. Pickens, Jr. Orangeburg, S.C. December 1, 1972	garden plan
687.	Mr. and Mrs. J. W. Pickens, Jr. Orangeburg, S.C. December 1, 1972	garden plan
688.	Mr. and Mrs. J. W. Pickens, Jr. Orangeburg, S.C. January 21, 1969	garden plan
689.	Pink House Square Myrtle Beach, S.C. November 27, 1963	parking plan
690.	Pink House Square Myrtle Beach, S.C. December 3, 1963	parking plan
691.	Point Farm Wadmalaw Island Charleston, S.C. January 8, 1965	plat for subdivision of tract
692.	House for lot no. 2, block 15 Beacon Hill Port Washington, N.Y. no date	north elevation
693.	House for lot no. 2, block 15 Beacon Hill Port Washington, N.Y. no date	second-floor plan
694.	House for lot no. 2, block 15 Beacon Hill Port Washington, N.Y. no date	elevations

REF. NO.	ORIGINAL OWNER / LOCATION	AVAILABLE INFORMATION
695.	House for lot no. 2, block 15 Beacon Hill Port Washington, N.Y. no date	first-floor plan
696.	Willis D. Porter Pleasantville, N.Y. December 5, 1921	profiles of landscape arrangements
697.	W. D. Porter Pleasantville, N.Y. no date	pergola
698.	W. D. Porter Pleasantville, N.Y. May 8, 1923	details of walls and gates
699.	Willis D. Porter, Esq. Pleasantville, N.Y. 1923	grading and construction plan
700.	Willis D. Porter, Esq. Pleasantville, N.Y. July 9, 1925	perennial garden
701.	Willis D. Porter, Esq. Pleasantville, N.Y. no date	planting plan
702.	Willis D. Porter, Esq. Pleasantville, N.Y. no date	preliminary planting plan
703.	Mr. and Mrs. Sherrill Poulnot The Crescent Charleston, S.C. February 3, 1961	general plan of grounds and planting details with field notes
704.	Mr. and Mrs. Sherrill Poulnot The Crescent Charleston, S.C. February 18, 1961	construction plan for grounds
705.	Mr. and Mrs. Sherrill Poulnot The Crescent Charleston, S.C. February 3, 1961	general plan of grounds
706.	Mr. and Mrs. Sherrill Poulnot The Crescent Charleston, S.C. February 20, 1961	general plan of grounds and planting details
707.	Mr. and Mrs. Sherrill Poulnot The Crescent Charleston, S.C. February 20, 1961	general plans of grounds and planting details

REF. NO.	ORIGINAL OWNER / LOCATION	AVAILABLE INFORMATION
708.	Mr. and Mrs. Sherrill Poulnot The Crescent Charleston, S.C. February 10, 1961	construction plan for grounds
709.	Presbyterian Home for the Aged Summerville, S.C. January 23, 1967	construction plan of garden
710.	Presbyterian Home for the Aged (2) Summerville, S.C. June 26, 1967	planting plan of garden
711.	Presbyterian Home for the Aged Summerville, S.C. January 23, 1967	construction plan—fountain and garden
712.	Presbyterian manse Rivers St. Lake City, S.C. February 28, 1969	planting plan
713.	Mr. Howard Prettyman Summerville, S.C. February 26, 1954	general landscape plan
714.	Mr. Howard Prettyman Summerville, S.C. no date	general landscape plan
715.	Primrose House East Bay Charleston, S.C. January 31, 1961	plan of grounds
716.	Mr. and Mrs. Ashmead F. Pringle, Jr. 32 South Battery Charleston, S.C. no date	construction plan of garden
717.	Ashmead Pringle, Esq. no date	sketch gardens
718.	Dr. and Mrs. W. H. Prioleau Mt. Pleasant, S.C. December 27, 1948	plan of wall and walks
719.	Dr. and Mrs. W. H. Prioleau Mt. Pleasant, S.C. January 11, 1949	plan of road and planting
720.	Dr. and Mrs. W. H. Prioleau Mt. Pleasant, S.C. January 11, 1949	plan of road, walks. and grading
721.	Dr. and Mrs. William Prioleau 82 King St. Charleston, S.C. February 19, 1960	construction plan of drive

REF. NO.	ORIGINAL OWNER / LOCATION	AVAILABLE INFORMATION
722.	2 Prioleau St. Charleston, S.C. November 8, 1967	planting plan for parking court
723.	Mrs. Edward K. Pritchard 58 Tradd St. Charleston, S.C. May 27, 1941	sketch plan of garden
724.	Prospect Hills School Hudson St. Pelham, N.Y. December, 1932	general plan of grounds
725.	Dr. and Mrs. Bert Pruitt, Jr. 54 Meeting St. Charleston, S.C. May 5, 1975	plan and elevations
726.	Dr. and Mrs. Bert Pruitt, Jr. 54 Meeting St. Charleston, S.C. May 5, 1975	construction plan for garden
727.	Public Works Administration Charleston, S.C. October 25, 1935	outline—preliminary site plan no. 8901-B
728.	Public Works Administration Housing Division, USA Charleston, S.C. April 7, 1936	planting plan—block 1
729.	Public Works Administration Housing Division, USA Charleston, S.C. April 7, 1936	planting plan—block 5
730.	Public Works Administration Housing Division, USA Charleston, S.C. April 7, 1936	planting plan—block 6
731.	Public Works Administration Housing Division, USA Charleston, S.C. April 7, 1936	planting plan—block 2 and 3
732.	Public Works Administration Housing Division, USA Charleston, S.C. April 7, 1936	planting plan—block 4
733.	Mr. and Mrs. James E. Ragsdale Lake City, S.C. January 17, 1960	landscape design

REF. NO.	ORIGINAL OWNER / LOCATION	AVAILABLE INFORMATION
734.	Mr. and Mrs. James Ragsdale Lake City, S.C. January 18, 1969	landscape plan
735.	Mr. and Mrs. T. S. Ragsdale Exchange Plantation Plantersville, S.C. February 14, 1946	construction and planting plan of garden
736.	T. S. Ragsdale, Esq. Exchange Plantation March 14, 1946	proposed gates at Exchange Plantation
737.	Mr. and Mrs. T. S. Ragsdale Exchange Plantation Plantersville, S.C. November 25, 1947	herb garden
738.	Mr. and Mrs. T. S. Ragsdale, Jr. Lake City, S.C. February 27, 1961	landscape design
739.	Mr. and Mrs. T. S. Ragsdale, Jr. Bowen St. Lake City, S.C. November 21, 1963	house location and general plan
740.	Mr. and Mrs. T. S. Ragsdale, Jr. Bowen St. Lake City, S.C. November 21, 1963	house location and general plan
741.	Mr. and Mrs. T. S. Ragsdale, Jr. Bowen St. Lake City, S.C. no date	site plan
742.	Mr. and Mrs. T. S. Ragsdale, Jr. Bowen St. Lake City, S.C. January 29, 1965	sketch of gates
743.	Mr. and Mrs. T. S. Ragsdale, Jr. Bowen St. Lake City, S.C. January 29, 1965	sketch of gates
744.	Mr. and Mrs. T. S. Ragsdale, Jr. Bowen St. Lake City, S.C. January 29, 1965	planting plan
745.	Mr. and Mrs. T. S. Ragsdale, Jr. Bowen St. Lake City, S.C. January 29, 1965	planting plan

REF. NO.	ORIGINAL OWNER / LOCATION	AVAILABLE INFORMATION
746.	Dr. J. H. Reed Bronxville, N.Y. no date	general plan
747.	Dr. J. H. Reed Bronxville, N.Y. no date	gate
748.	Mr. and Mrs. Graham Reeves Charleston, S.C. June 26, 1967	elevations of residence
749.	Mr. and Mrs. Graham Reeves Charleston, S.C. June 29, 1967	elevations of residence
750.	Mr. and Mrs. Graham Reeves Charleston, S.C. June 23, 1967	environmental design
751.	Mr. and Mrs. Graham Reeves Charleston, S.C. June 27, 1967	sheet no. 2 of 4—floor plans
752.	Mr. and Mrs. Graham Reeves (3) Tradd St. Charleston, S.C. June 12, 1968	preliminary plans
753.	Mr. and Mrs. William Reeves Charleston, S.C. January 8, 1968	construction plan of grounds with field notes
754.	Mr. and Mrs. William Reeves Charleston, S.C. January 2, 1968	construction plan of grounds
755.	Mr. and Mrs. William Reeves Charleston, S.C. March 1, 1968	entrance post
756.	Mr. and Mrs. William Reeves Charleston, S.C. June 23, 1967	environmental design with field notes
757.	Mr. and Mrs. William Reeves Tradd St. Charleston, S.C. no date	planting plan and drive plan with field notes
758.	Mr. and Mrs. William Reeves Tradd St. Charleston, S.C. January 8, 1968	construction plan of grounds with field notes
759.	Mr. and Mrs. Graham Reeves 109 Tradd St. Charleston, S.C. no date	first-floor plan

REF. NO.	ORIGINAL OWNER / LOCATION	AVAILABLE INFORMATION
760.	Mr. and Mrs. Graham Reeves 109 Tradd St. Charleston, S.C. no date	west elevation
761.	Mr. and Mrs. Graham Reeves 109 Tradd St. Charleston, S.C. no date	north or front elevation
762.	Mr. and Mrs. Graham Reeves 109 Tradd St. Charleston, S.C. no date	second-floor plan
763.	Mr. and Mrs. Graham Reeves 109 Tradd St. Charleston, S.C. no date	bedroom floor
764.	Mr. and Mrs. Graham Reeves 109 Tradd St. Charleston, S.C. no date	east elevation
765.	Mr. and Mrs. Graham Reeves 109 Tradd St. Charleston, S.C. December 11, 1967	preliminary plan of grounds
766.	Mr. and Mrs. Graham Reeves 109 Tradd St. Charleston, S.C. March 1, 1968	entrance post
767.	Mr. and Mrs. Graham Reeves 109 Tradd St. Charleston, S.C. February 16, 1968	planting plan and drive plan
768.	Residential environment no location February 19, 1965	three arrangements for low-cost housing
769.	Residential environment no location no date	rough layout for three arrangements for low-cost housing
770.	Residential environment no date	three basic requirements
771.	Mr. and Mrs. R. J. Reynolds Winston-Salem, N.C. January 23, 1919	planting plan about basin for irrigation system
772.	Mrs. R. Barnwell Rhett 48 Murray Blvd. Charleston, S.C. January 21, 1964	construction drawings—drive, garage court, walks, and walls

REF. NO.	ORIGINAL OWNER / LOCATION	AVAILABLE INFORMATION
773.	Mrs. R. Barnwell Rhett 48 Murray Blvd. Charleston, S.C. January 21, 1964	construction drawings—drive, garage court, walks, and walls
774.	Mrs. Frederick Richards 100 Tradd St. Charleston, S.C. May 13, 1975	arbor in the garden
775.	Mrs. Frederick Richards 100 Tradd St. Charleston, S.C. no date	arbor arch detail
776.	Mr. and Mrs. Frederick Richards, Jr. 100 Tradd St. Charleston, S.C. no date	construction drawings for garden
777.	Mr. and Mrs. Warren Ripley 8 Orange St. Charleston, S.C. November 25, 1968	garden design
778.	Rip Van Winkle Lake and Recreation Park Tannersville, N.Y. April 10, 1936	general grading plan
779.	Rip Van Winkle Lake and Recreation Park Tannersville, N.Y. April 10, 1936	general grading plan
780.	Dr. and Mrs. Arthur L. Rivers 42 S. Battery St. Charleston, S.C. May 21, 1947	garden design
781.	L. Mendel Rivers monument (2) Charleston, S.C. May 18, 1971	preliminary study
782.	L. Mendel Rivers memorial Charleston, S.C. April 8, 1971	landscape design
783.	Mrs. W. A. Roebling 64 South Battery Charleston, S.C. February 26, 1929	alterations to residence
784.	Mrs. Washington Roebling 64 South Battery Charleston, S.C. June 11, 1929	gate with panels

REF. NO.	ORIGINAL OWNER / LOCATION	AVAILABLE INFORMATION
785.	Mrs. Washington Roebling 64 South Battery Charleston, S.C. no date	sketch of gate
786.	Mrs. Washington Roebling 64 South Battery Charleston, S.C. March 6, 1930	full-size details of two capitals—garden gate
787.	Mrs. Washington Roebling 64 South Battery Charleston, S.C. no date	full-size detail—base for lead figures—garden
788.	Mrs. Washington Roebling 64 South Battery Charleston, S.C. December 8, 1930	sundial pedestal
789.	Mrs. Washington Roebling 64 South Battery Charleston, S.C. no date	full-size detail of pool coping
790.	Mrs. W. D. Rogers 47 Legare St. Charleston, S.C. no date	details of garden—porch and garden trellis
791.	Russell House no location April 9, 1967	sketch plan—new gardens
792.	Russell House Charleston, S.C. April 9, 1967	sketch plan—new gardens
793.	Nathaniel Russell House Charleston, S.C. October 25, 1967	proposed paving
794.	Russell House Garden Charleston, S.C. June 12, 1969	base for four statues
795.	Nathaniel Russell House Charleston, S.C. October 25, 1967	proposed paving
796.	Nathaniel Russell House Charleston, S.C. May 29, 1970	outline of garden and recommended brick walk and flagstone terrace
797.	158 Rutledge Ave. Charleston, S.C. January 28, 1958	landscape plan

REF. NO.	ORIGINAL OWNER / LOCATION	AVAILABLE INFORMATION
798.	160 Rutledge Ave. Charleston, S.C. April 18, 1956	three location plans for proposed buildings
799.	Ryedale Farm Accabee, S.C. surveyed March 1905	photograph of site plan
800.	St. Andrews Church St. Andrews Parish Charleston Co., S.C. October 1, 1949	map of a part of the land
801.	St. Andrews Churchyard St. Andrews Parish Charleston Co., S.C. March 24, 1951	map
802.	Old. St. Andrews Cemetery Charleston Co., S.C. April 16, 1951	plan
803.	Old St. Andrews Cemetery St. Andrews Parish Charleston Co., S.C. no date	preliminary plan
804.	St. Andrews Churchyard Wardens of the Parish of St. Andrews Charleston Co., S.C. December 6, 1952	map of the north portion of the church tract
805.	St. Andrews Churchyard Wardens of the Parish of St. Andrews Charleston Co., S.C. March 26, 1951	map—portion of with tree locations
806.	St. Andrews Churchyard Wardens of the Parish of St. Andrews Charleston Co., S.C. March 26, 1951	map—portion of with plantings
807.	St. Andrews Charleston Co., S.C. March 26, 1951	churchyard
808.	Old St. Andrews Cemetery, West Section St. Andrews Charleston Co., S.C. July 22, 1955	preliminary plan no. 2
809.	Eastern Cemetery of St. Philips Church Church St. Charleston S.C. April 1932	plat map
810.	Western Cemetery of St. Philips Church Charleston, S.C. April 1932	plat plan

REF. NO.	ORIGINAL OWNER / LOCATION	AVAILABLE INFORMATION
811.	St. Philips Cemetery Charleston, S.C. June 16, 1967	alternate fence design for low wall
812.	St. Philips Cemetery Charleston, S.C. June 16, 967	alternate fence designs
813.	Western Cemetery, St. Philips Church St. Charleston, S.C. November 20, 1967	plans for walks and iron fence
814.	Mr. and Mrs. H. C. Schackelford 97 East Bay Charleston, S.C. November 25, 1968	garden design
815.	Mr. and Mrs. H. C. Schackelford 97 East Bay Charleston, S.C. November 25, 1968	garden design
816.	Dr. S. T. Scarborough 12 King St. Charleston, S.C. June 16, 1966	construction plan, wall, and drive location
817.	Dr. S. T. Scarborough 12 King St. Charleston, S.C. June 16, 1966	construction plan—wall and drive entrance
818.	Mr. and Mrs. H. C. Shackelford Wideawake Plantation March 23, 1960	plan of patio garden
819.	Mr. and Mrs. Herbert J. Scholz Summerville, S.C. October 28, 1968	plan of construction and planting
820.	Schuyler and Lounsbery 1409 Twentieth St., NW Washington, D.C.	city garden
821.	Mrs. Holton Scott Pelham, N.Y. November 1, 1926	planting plan of garden
822.	Mr. and Mrs. Rudolph Siegling Charleston, S.C. August 21, 1947	garden plan—detail of rear wall
823.	Mr. and Mrs. J. Simons 15 Church Street Charleston, S.C. April 3, 1946	garden design

REF. NO.	ORIGINAL OWNER / LOCATION	AVAILABLE INFORMATION
824.	Mr. and Mrs. Huger Sinkler Charleston, S.C. February 6, 1959	plan no. 3—construction and planting of garden
825.	Mr. and Mrs. Huger Sinkler Charleston, S.C. January 9, 1959	general plan of garden
826.	Mr. and Mrs. Huger Sinkler 39 Church St. Charleston, S.C. December 4, 1958	planting no. 1—planting at front
827.	Mrs. Huger Sinkler 8½ Exchange St. Charleston, S.C. February 9–10, 1965	plant bed, preliminary study
828.	Mr. and Mrs. Huger Sinkler Rosebank March 29, 1962	revised plan of garden and drive
829.	Mr. and Mrs. J. H. Small 26 Church St. Charleston, S.C. October 17, 1967	floor plan
830.	Mr. and Mrs. James H. Small 26 Church St. Charleston, S.C. no date	landscape plan
831.	Mr. and Mrs. James H. Small 26 Church St. Charleston, S.C. no date	landscape plan
832.	Mr. and Mrs. James H. Small 26 Church St. Charleston, S.C. no date	landscape plan
833.	Mr. and Mrs. James H. Small 26 Church St. Charleston, S.C. no date	plat
834.	Mrs. W. Aimar Smith 30 Council St. Charleston, S.C. January 28, 1957	planting plan
835.	Mr. and Mrs. A. T. Smythe, Jr. 25 State St. Charleston, S.C. April 4, 1960	plan of garden

REF. NO.	ORIGINAL OWNER / LOCATION	AVAILABLE INFORMATION
836.	Mr. and Mrs. A. T. Smythe, Jr. 0 Gibbes St. Charleston, S.C. February 21, 1966	second-floor plan
837.	Mr. and Mrs. A. T. Smythe, Jr. 0 Gibbes St. Charleston, S.C. July 21, 1965	remodeling
838.	Mr. and Mrs. A. T. Smythe, Jr. 0 Gibbes St. Charleston, S.C. December 7, 1966	preliminary site plan
839.	Mr. and Mrs. A. T. Smythe, Jr. 0 Gibbes St. Charleston, S.C. January 31, 1969	garage and workshop
840.	Mr. and Mrs. A. T. Smythe, Jr. 0 Gibbes St. Charleston, S.C. November 30, 1967	sketches of utility building
841.	Mr. and Mrs. A. T. Smythe, Jr. 0 Gibbes St. Charleston, S.C. no date	plan and elevations of garage/summerhouse
842.	No name 0 Gibbes St. Charleston, S.C. no date	sketch—playroom and garage
843.	Mr. and Mrs. Henry B. Smythe 35 Legare St. Charleston, S.C. June 6, 1961	plan of grounds
844.	The South Carolina Garden Club Memorial Garden Lincoln and Calhoun Sts. Columbia, S.C. April 3, 1946	general design
845.	South Carolina National Bank 16 Broad St. Charleston, S.C. November 17, 1971	construction drawings— additions to parking area
846.	South Carolina National Bank 16 Broad Street Charleston, S.C. November 17, 1971	construction drawings— additions to parking area

REF. NO.	ORIGINAL OWNER / LOCATION	AVAILABLE INFORMATION
847.	South Carolina National Bank 16 Broad Street Charleston, S.C. no date	plans by town and country landscaping
848.	South Carolina National Bank 16 Broad Street Charleston, S.C. January 20, 1972	planting plan
849.	South Carolina National Bank 16 Broad Street Charleston, S.C. March 15, 1972	plan of additional construction details and irrigation system
850.	Mr. and Mrs. Clarence Southwood 155 Beechwood Rd. Ridgewood, N.J. May 17, 1955	landscape plan
851.	Mr. and Mrs. Henry P. Staats 59 Church St. Charleston, S.C. July 15, 1954	construction plan of grounds
852.	Mr. and Mrs. Henry P. Staats 59 Church St. Charleston, S.C. February 17, 1954	sketch plan—site development
853.	Mrs. H. Phillip Staats 62 Church St. Charleston, S.C. August 5, 1974	plan no. 1—grounds west end of property
854.	Mrs. H. Phillip Staats 62 Church St. Charleston, S.C. November 1974	plan no. 2 of 2—garden construction and planting
855.	Mrs. H. Phillip Staats 62 Church St. Charleston, S.C. November 2, 1974	plan no. 2 of 2—garden construction and planting
856.	Mrs. H. Phillip Staats 62 Church St. Charleston, S.C. August 5, 1974	plan no. 1—grounds west end of property
857.	Mrs. H. Phillip Staats 54 Church St. Charleston, S.C. no date	remodeling and additions to a dwelling at 62 Church St.

REF. NO.	ORIGINAL OWNER / LOCATION	AVAILABLE INFORMATION
858.	Mrs. H. Phillip Staats 59 Church St. Charleston, S.C. December 16, 1972	remodeling and additions to a dwelling at 62 Church St.
859.	Mrs. H. Phillip Staats 54 Church St. Charleston, S.C. no date	existing first and second floor
860.	Roger Steffan, Esq. Eagle Hommocks Mamaroneck, N.Y. no date	construction plan of garden
861.	Roger Steffan, Esq. Eagle Hommocks Mamaroneck, N.Y. no date	planting plan of garden
862.	Mr. and Mr. Herbert R. Stender, Jr. 64 Church Street Charleston, S.C. May 26, 1961	landscape plan
863.	Mr. and Mrs. Thomas C. Stevenson, Jr. 2 S. Battery Charleston, S.C. June 17, 1963	garden plan
864.	Strawberry Chapel Charleston, S.C. March 16, 1944	construction details
865.	Mr. Homer Sullivan Pelham Wood Westchester Co., N.Y. no date	residence
866.	Summerville Baptist Church Summerville, S.C. February 17, 1949	landscape plan
867.	Summit, N.J. July 20, 1936	preliminary plan—alt no. 1
868.	Summit, N.J. July 17, 1936	preliminary plan—alt no. 2
869.	F. C. Sutro, Esq. Basking Ridge, N.J. November 18, 1922	sketch plan
870.	F. C. Sutro, Esq. Basking Ridge, N.J. November 24, 1922	sketch of garden
871.	Frederick C. Sutro, Esq. Basking Ridge, N.J. September 10, 1923	perennial plan for pergola

REF. NO.	ORIGINAL OWNER / LOCATION	AVAILABLE INFORMATION
872.	Frederick C. Sutro, Esq. Basking Ridge, N.J. no date	planting plan for garden
873.	Edwin H. Sutterwaite, Esq. Doylestown, Pa. November 9, 1950	plan for grading and construction
874.	Edwin H. Sutterwaite, Esq. Doylestown, Pa. November 9, 1950	plan for grading and construction
875.	W. Carsten Wulbern 33 State Street Charleston, S.C. no date	plan of rear and side yards
876.	W. Carsten Wulbern 33 State Street Charleston, S.C. February 21, 1962	site plan
877.	Mrs. E. J. Thornhill James Island, S.C. February 19, 1946	construction and planting plan
878.	109 Tradd St. Charleston, S.C. June 14, 1967	plat
879.	1 Tradd St. Charleston, S.C. December 26, 1963	curb drainage and paving plan
880.	Trinity-Grace Church Springfield, Mass. January 2, 1924	planting plan
881.	Tulane University New Orleans, La. no date	library building plan
882.	Tulane University New Orleans, La. no date	brick and wall details
883.	Mr. Wilbur H. Vandine Doylestown, Pa. August 2, 1946	sketch plan
884.	Mr. Wilbur H. Vandine Doylestown, Pa. no date	rendered sketch of office steps
885.	Mr. Wilbur H. Vandine Doylestown, Pa. August 5, 1952	construction details—office entrance

REF. NO.	ORIGINAL OWNER / LOCATION	AVAILABLE INFORMATION
886.	Villa Gamberaia no location no date	plan view
887.	Mr. and Mrs. D. C. Waddell, Jr. Chicora Wood June 14, 1938	details of terrace and walks
888.	Mr. and Mrs. Hugh Walker 10 King St. Charleston, S.C. January 13, 1966	powder room
889.	Mr. and Mrs. Hugh Walker 10 King St. Charleston, S.C. November 24, 1965	plan—relocation of stair and proposed washroom
890.	Mr. and Mrs. Hugh Walker 10 King St. Charleston, S.C. April 1, 1966	entrance
891.	Mr. and Mrs. Hugh Walker 10 King St. Charleston, S.C. no date	wrought-iron gate
892.	Mr. and Mrs. Hugh Walker 10 King St. Charleston, S.C. June 5, 1963	general plan of grounds
893.	Mr. and Mrs. Hugh Walker 10 King St. Charleston, S.C. November 24, 1965	construction plan of garden
894.	Mr. and Mrs. Hugh Walker 10 King St. Charleston, S.C. November 24, 1965	construction plan of garden with field notes
895.	Mr. and Mrs. Hugh Walker 10 King St. Charleston, S.C. January 5, 1966	kitchen plan
896.	Mr. and Mrs. Hugh Walker 10 King St. Charleston, S.C. April 1, 1966	entrance with field notes
897.	Mr. and Mrs. Hugh Walker 10 King St. Charleston, S.C. April 1, 1966	entrance

REF. NO.	ORIGINAL OWNER / LOCATION	AVAILABLE INFORMATION
898.	Mrs. Craig Wall Conway, S.C.	part of landscape design
899.	Mt. Pleasant, S.C. no date	showing plantation gardens
900.	W. W. Wannamaker, Jr., Esq. Orangeburg, S.C. February 3, 1931	foundation planting
901.	W. W. Wannamaker, Jr., Esq. Orangeburg, S.C. February 3, 1951	foundation planting
902.	W. W. Wannamaker, Jr., Esq. Orangeburg, S.C. December 15, 1948	sketch plan
903.	W. W. Wannamaker, Jr., Esq. Orangeburg, S.C. January 5, 1949	construction plan—grading, drives, walks, walls
904.	W. W. Wannamaker, Jr., Esq. Orangeburg, S.C. June 9, 1949	details—pavings, walls, posts, and steps
905.	W. W. Wannamaker, Jr., Esq. Orangeburg, S.C. January 5, 1949	construction plan with field notes
906.	Mr. and Mrs. W. W. Wannamaker, Jr. Orangeburg, S.C. April 29, 1949	details of wrought-iron railings and brick patterns
907.	W. W. Wannamaker, Jr., Esq. Orangeburg, S.C. September 28, 1949	garden gate
908.	Mr. W. W. Wannamaker, Jr. 703 Kirkwood Cir. Camden, S.C. December 29, 1953	plan—site development
909.	Mr. and Mrs. W. W. Wannamaker, Jr. Orangeburg, S.C. February 8, 1954	plan for terrace and plan for rose garden
910.	Mr. W. W. Wannamaker III 703 Kirkwood Cir. Camden, S.C. March 2, 1954	planting plan
911.	Wannamaker Family Plot Orangeburg, S.C. February 20, 1957	landscape design
912.	War Housing Project Charleston, S.C. February 10, 1943	block no. 1, SC-38069-B (landscape)

REF. NO.	ORIGINAL OWNER / LOCATION	AVAILABLE INFORMATION
913.	War Memorial Doylestown, Pa. October 23, 1945	proposed site
914.	Memorial field and high school grounds Doylestown, Pa. November 19, 1945	sketch no. 1
915.	War Memorial Field Doylestown, Pa. July 29, 1947	location plan for baseball field house
916.	War Memorial Field Doylestown, Pa. June 6, 1946	sketch plan of grading and construction
917.	War Memorial Field Doylestown, Pa. May 17, 1946	preliminary plan no. 2
918.	War Memorial Field Doylestown, Pa. July 29, 1947	location plan for baseball field and field house
919.	War Memorial Field Doylestown, Pa. June 6, 1946	sketch plan of grading and construction
920.	War Memorial Field Doylestown, Pa. Upper State Road June 25, 1946	grading plan
921.	War Memorial Field Doylestown, Pa. June 25, 1946	grading plan with field notes
922.	War Memorial Field Doylestown, Pa. June 25, 1946	grading plan
923.	War Memorial Field Doylestown, Pa. July 11, 1947	general plan for entrance and parking
924.	Mr. and Mrs. D. C. Wardell Chicora Wood January 24, 1947	construction plan of entrance gate
925.	Mrs. Simon V. H. Waring 46 King St. Charleston, S.C. October 14, 1965	garden gate and door
926.	Mr. V. H. Waring 10 King St. Charleston, S.C.	drive and curbs

REF. NO.	ORIGINAL OWNER / LOCATION	AVAILABLE INFORMATION
927.	Mrs. W. W. Warner Pelham	sketch of lattice and gate
928.	Mrs. W. W. Warner Pelham, N.Y. March 27, 1925	planting plan
929.	Col. and Mrs. Charles Watson Bull St. Charleston, S.C. May 10, 1975	landscape plan no. 1
930.	Col. and Mrs. Charles Watson Bull St. Charleston, S.C. May 12, 1975	plan of pool—fountain, walk, drive, and parking area—south end of site
931.	Col. and Mrs. Charles Watson Bull St. Charleston, S.C. May 10, 1975	landscape plan no. 1
932.	Col. and Mrs. Charles Watson Bull St. Charleston, S.C. May 12, 1975	plan of pool—fountain, walk, drive, and parking area—south end of site
933.	Col. and Mrs. Charles Watson Bull St. Charleston, S.C. March 1975	preliminary plan no. 2—south end of site
934.	Col. and Mrs. Charles Watson Charleston, S.C. March 1975	preliminary plan no. 2—south end of site with field notes
935.	Mr. and Mrs. Norman H. Watt 65 King Street Charleston, S.C. October 30, 1967	site plan
936.	Mrs. Weitzel 16 Elliot St. Charleston, S.C. January 31, 1961	garden plan
937.	Mr. and Mrs. John T. Welch, Jr. 29 Legare St. Charleston, S.C. April 4, 1968	sketch of bathhouse and brick construction
938.	Mr. and Mrs. John T. Welch, Jr. 29 Legare St. Charleston, S.C. May 14, 1968	revised walk and parking area

REF. NO.	ORIGINAL OWNER / LOCATION	AVAILABLE INFORMATION
939.	Mr. and Mrs. John T. Welch, Jr. 29 Legare St. Charleston, S.C. May 16, 1968	design no. 2
940.	Mr. and Mrs. John T. Welch, Jr. 29 Legare St. Charleston, S.C. April 4, 1968	sketch of bathhouse and brick construction
941.	Mr. and Mrs. John T. Welch, Jr. 29 Legare St. Charleston, S.C. April 4, 1968	sketch of bathhouse and brick construction
942.	Mr. and Mrs. John T. Welch, Jr. 29 Legare St. Charleston, S.C. May 16, 1968	design no. 2—walk and parking areas
943.	L. R. Wells, Jr. Orangeburg, S.C. September 19, 1967	rendered preliminary plan— drives and gardens
944.	Mr. and Mrs. Lawrence R. Wells Orangeburg, S.C. December 5, 1958	landscape plan
945.	L. R. Wells, Jr. Wells Dr. Orangeburg, S.C. September 19, 1967	preliminary plan—drives and gardens
946.	Mr. and Mrs. Lawrence R. Wells, Jr. Orangeburg, S.C. October 14, 1967	garden plan
947.	L. R. Wells, Jr. Orangeburg, S.C. October 20, 1967	general plan and drive location
948.	Mr. and Mrs. Lawrence R. Wells, Jr. Wells Drive Orangeburg, S.C. no date	floor plans, finishes, elevations, sections
949.	Mr. and Mrs. Lawrence Wells Orangeburg, S.C. May 9, 1950	general construction plan
950.	Mr. and Mrs. Lawrence Wells Orangeburg, S.C. March 1, 1951	general plan
951.	Mr. and Mrs. Eugene West Marion, S.C. February 2, 1956	location of front drive and parking

REF. NO.	ORIGINAL OWNER / LOCATION	AVAILABLE INFORMATION
952.	Mr. and Mrs. Ben Scott Whaley 58 Church St. Charleston, S.C. January 25, 1965	construction details—west end of garden
953.	Mrs. Ben Scott Whaley 58 Church St. Charleston, S.C.	sketch plan of garden
954.	Mrs. Wichmann Pitt and Montagu Sts. Charleston, S.C. May 29, 1964	general plan of grounds
955.	Mr. and Mrs. E. Lloyd Willcox 2 King St. Charleston, S.C. November 27, 1951	planting plan
956.	Mr. and Mrs. E. Lloyd Willcox 2 King St. Charleston, S.C. April 20, 1950	construction plan—garden and drainage
957.	A. E. Widli, Esq. Willets Ave. White Plains, N.Y. no date	road plan
958.	Mrs. Churchill Williams Spring Meadow Farm Gardenville, Pa. November 5, 1945	construction plan—garden
959.	Mr. and Mrs. Rodney Williams 72 Anson St. Charleston, S.C. September 12, 1970	construction and planting plan of grounds
960.	Mr. and Mrs. Rodney Williams 72 Anson St. Charleston, S.C. September 12, 1970	construction and planting plan of grounds
961.	Williamsburg style December 26, 1963	fence and gate
962.	Williamsburg style December 26, 1963	fence and gate
963.	Dr. and Mrs. Robert Wilson 43 King St. Charleston, S.C. January 12, 1955	planting plan of front yard
964.	Dr. and Mrs. Robert Wilson 43 King St. Charleston, S.C. May 1, 1975	garden wall

REF. NO.	ORIGINAL OWNER / LOCATION	AVAILABLE INFORMATION
965.	Woodbrook Estates (Bitzer) Doylestown, Pa. November 10, 1953	preliminary plan of subdivision
966.	Woodbrook Estates (Bitzer) Doylestown, Pa. November 3, 1953	preliminary plan of subdivision
967.	Mr. and Mrs. Perry Woods 93 Church St. Charleston, S.C. March 10, 1961	plan of garden
968.	Woodside Park Stamford, Conn. March 5, 1928	general plan
969.	Woodside Park Stamford, Conn. March 5, 1928	general plan
970.	Mr. and Mrs. Charles H. Woodward 14 Rutledge Ave. Charleston, S.C. December 5, 1962	general plan of grounds, no. 2, and construction plan
971.	Mr. and Mrs. Charles H. Woodward 14 Rutledge Ave. Charleston, S.C. December 5, 1962	general plan of grounds, no. 2, and construction plan
972.	Mr. and Mrs. Charles H. Woodward 94 Rutledge Ave. Charleston, S.C. May 29, 1964	construction details—walls and fountain
973.	Mr. and Mrs. Charles H. Woodward 94 Rutledge Ave. Charleston, S.C. May 29, 1964	construction details—wall and fountain
974.	Elizabeth Gadsen Woodward Adgers Wharf Park Charleston, S.C. no date	landscape plan—planting specification
975.	W. Carsten Wulbern 33 State St. Charleston, S.C. no date	plan of rear and side yards
976.	Yeamans Hall N. Charleston, S.C. May 23, 1967	preliminary landscape plan with field notes
977.	Yeamans Hall N. Charleston, S.C. May 23, 1967	landscape plan

REF. NO.	ORIGINAL OWNER / LOCATION	AVAILABLE INFORMATION
978.	Yeamans Hall N. Charleston, S.C. May 23, 1967	patio and pool
979.	Yeamans Hall N. Charleston, S.C. September 22, 1967	planting plan and paving
980.	Yeamans Hall Club N. Charleston, S.C. August 1925	colored general plan by Olmsted Brothers
981.	Yeamans Hall Club N. Charleston, S.C. October 25, 1967	plan for grounds
982.	Yeamans Hall tract Goose Creek Berkeley Co., S.C. May 31, 1967	proposed layout
983.	Edith H. Yewell Town of Hillsdale Col. Co. N.Y. June 12, 1964	subdivision plat
984.	Edith H. Yewell Town of Hillsdale Col. Co., N.Y. June 19, 1963	subdivision plat
985.	J. Floyd Yewell Town of Hillsdale Col. Co., N.Y. March 27, 1957	plat map
986.	J. Floyd Yewell Town of Hillsdale Col. Co., N.Y. no date	subdivision
987.	Mr. and Mrs. J. Floyd Yewell Hillsdale, N.Y. September 2, 1954	landscape plan
988.	Mr. and Mrs. J. Floyd Yewell Hillsdale, N.Y. August 16, 1957	plan of woodland garden
989.	Mr. and Mrs. Joseph R. Young Charleston, S.C. October 16, 1959	sketch of fountain and terrace
990.	Mr. and Mrs. Joseph R. Young Charleston, S.C. November 6, 1959	garden construction plan

REF. NO.	ORIGINAL OWNER / LOCATION	AVAILABLE INFORMATION
991.	Mr. and Mrs. Joseph R. Young 70 Tradd Street Charleston, S.C. February 13, 1967	construction plan—terrace, pool, and wall
992.	Mr. and Mrs. Joseph R. Young 70 Tradd Street Charleston, S.C. March 23, 1967	construction plan
993.	Mr. J. Conrad Zimmerman Summerville, S.C. December 11, 1959	sketch of terrace

Unknowns and Maps

994.	Edward Fennwick Stono River (location not marked) no date	photostat of plat map
995.	Reversed photostat Mouth of Ashley River property no date	boundary survey
996.	Two identical photostats Branch of Stono River no date	old property survey
997.	Princeton Princeton University no date	plat map
998.	USGS Map March 1892	Maine Gardener sheet
999.	USGS Map March 1892	Maine Augusta sheet
1000.	Strawberry data no date	photostat of stone rubbing
1001.	East side of Anson Street Between Laurens and Society Streets Charleston, S.C. August 7, 1959	plat map
1002.	Site inventory no date	first-floor plan
1003.	No name no date	terrace plan and wall elevation
1004.	No name no location no date	full-size detail of ironwork

REF. NO.	ORIGINAL OWNER / LOCATION	AVAILABLE INFORMATION
1005.	No name no location no date	ironwork detail—full size and scaled
1006.	No name no location no date	first-floor plan by Melvin F. Gay, AIA, comm no.5502, sheet no. 3
1007.	No name no location no date	grounds plan with housing (ink)
1008.	No name no location no date	cemetery plots (ink)
1009.	No name no location no date	new town layout(?)
1010.	No name no location no date	elevation of house, Tudor style
1011.	No name no location no date	rendered topography and street locations
1012.	No name no location no date	road, drive, and property plan with existing trees
1013.	No name no location no date	enlargement of road, drive, property plan with existing trees
1014.	No name no location no date	full-size ironwork fence detail
1015.	Lee Perry, Architect no location no date	plan and landscape plan of tower
1016.	No name no location no date	full-scale drawing of ironwork (brown paper and 24" × 72")
1017.	No name no location no date	site plan—planting driveway pencil on back of old print
1018.	No name November 27, 1943	study no. 2—house made from four crates
1019.	No name no location no date	details of pool at north of grounds— plan sections

REF. NO.	ORIGINAL OWNER / LOCATION	AVAILABLE INFORMATION
1020.	No name no location no date	four rendered elevations with building facades, perhaps Murray-LaSaine Elementary School
1021.	No name no location no date	highway details—construction
1022.	No name no location no date	preliminary house and grounds location
1023.	No name no location no date	elevation of connected two story and nine story buildings
1024.	No name no location no date	section of roof framing and belfry
1025.	No name no location no date	wall and gate details—brick wall west end of house and brick wall—east end of house
1026.	Huguenin—Ragsdale—Whaley no date (but after August 9, 1965)	sketch plan of drive and/or garden
1027.	No name no date	plans for house
1028.	No name no date	contour map—seven feet long
1029.	No name (job no. 5812) no location (A. E. Constantine) no date	elevations and sections of building (A. E. Constantine)
1030.	No name (project no. 6802) (Curtis and Davis Architects) no date	north elevation
1031.	No name no location October 7, 1959	elevations and floor plans of building
1032.	5 Water St. no date	site plan
1033.	No name no date	floor plans
1034.	No name no date	yard plan
1035.	No name no date	perspective drawing of garden
1036.	No name no date	roof framing plan and detail

REF. NO.	ORIGINAL OWNER / LOCATION	AVAILABLE INFORMATION
1037.	No name no date	lintel and porch section
1038.	No name no date	plans and sections of steps and ramped steps
1039.	10 King St. Charleston, S.C. June 22, 1966	sketch of door hood construction plans— drive and walk—north wall
1040.	Frank Elwood Briggs MDCCCLXXXIII	diploma
1041.*	Loutrel Winslow Briggs Ithaca, N.Y. June 27, 1917	Cornell University diploma
1041.	No name no date	detail of garden plan and site planting plan
1042.	No name no date	topography map with house location
1043.	No name no date	details of picket fence
1044.	No name no date	sketch of suggested treatment for brick buildings
1045.	No name no date	post-top detail
1046.	No name no date	sections of brick wall
1047.	No name no date	sketch of rose arbor fence and gate detail
1048.	No name no date	door elevation and section/plan
1049.	No name no date	sections and elevations of house
1050.	No name no date	garden gates with elevation and side elevation
1051.	Middleton Plantation Charleston, S.C.	photograph—negative
1052.	College of Charleston St. Philip St. no date	site plan for parking at student union / dormitory
1053.	No name no date	detail sections of pool
1054.	No name no date	paving patterns
1055.	Algo	crossword for LA's

*Two listings are numbered "1041."

REF. NO.	ORIGINAL OWNER / LOCATION	AVAILABLE INFORMATION
1056.	L. W. Briggs no date	crossword for LA's
1057.	Villa Gamberaia no date	plan
1058.	Plan no. 2	garden pool, sundial base, lattice, sunroom steps
1059.	Railing detail no date	fence detail
1060.	Degree in Latin date in Latin	Collegii Haverfordiensis
1061.	Degree for Frank Briggs Haverford College June 6, 1883	Loganian Society
1062.	Office building Broad St. and Mechanic St. no date	plot plan
1063.	End of rail no date	sketch

Inventoried by David Utterback and given to the South Carolina Historical Society,
November 24, 1980.

Loutrel Briggs Archives at Historic Charleston Foundation

CLIENT	NAME OF PROPERTY / ADDRESS	DATE(S) OF DRAWING(S)	TITLE	SIZE (W" × L")
J. S. Frelinghuysen	Rice Hope Plantation, Oakley, S.C.	5/27/1929 (sketch plans); 5/27/1930 (construction plan)	construction plan of garden at Rice Hope Plantation	32 × 24.5
J. S. Frelinghuysen	Rice Hope Plantation	3/23/1932 and 5/26/1932	construction plan of garden at Rice Hope	23 × 22
J. S. Frelinghuysen	Rice Hope Plantation	undated	plan of planting at house	32 × 9.75
Not indicated	Rice Hope Plantation, Oakley, S.C.	undated	plan of stones for terrace	15 × 11.25
Not indicated	Rice Hope Plantation, Moncks Corner, S.C.	4/16/1936	memorandum of recommendations for planting at Rice Hope	16 × 26.5
Mr. and Mrs. Reginald Finke	Rice Hope Plantation	undated	additional planting for garden at Rice Hope	30.5 × 19.5
Mrs. W. Davis Rogers	47 Legare St., Charleston	undated	construction plan and details of garden	16.5 × 20.25
Mrs. W. Davis Rogers	47 Legare St., Charleston	5/23/1934	planting plan and pool details	14 × 18.5
Dr. and Mrs. Robert M. Hope	12 Meeting St., Charleston	11/25/1940	plan of garden	29 × 24.5
Not indicated	Strawberry Chapel	3/31/1944	marker of Strawberry Chapel	24 × 36
Not indicated	Strawberry Chapel	2/15/1944 and 4/2/1944	planting plan for plot at Strawberry Chapel	24 × 36
Mrs. Edwin Parsons	51 East Bay St. or 83 East Battery	11/21/1941	planting plan of garden	13 × 23.5
Mrs. Edwin Parsons	51 East Bay St. or 83 East Battery	6/10/1941, 6/20/1941	construction plan (addition) of garden	17.5 × 22.5
Mrs. Edward Ely	43 Tradd St.	11/23/1932	garden plan	23 × 13
Mrs. Vance C. McCormack	Belle Isle Plantation, Pineville	undated	planting design for entrance to tomb of General Francis Marion in S.C.	24.5 × 25.25
R. T. Edwards	Conway, S.C.	2/31/1941	construction details of pool	30.75 × 14.5
R. T. Edwards	Conway, S.C.	2/1/1941, rev'd 3/5/1941	planting plan no. 3	32.25 × 28

CLIENT	NAME OF PROPERTY / ADDRESS	DATE(S) OF DRAWING(S)	TITLE	SIZE (W" × L")
Clarence Chapman	Mulberry, Oakley	undated	full-size details for molded bricks for garden wall at Mulberry	12.5 × 14.5
Clarence Chapman	Mulberry	11/27/1931	full-size detail of limestone coping for pool at Mulberry	17.25 × 22.5
Clarence Chapman (Mrs.)	Mulberry, Oakley, S.C.	1/29/1931	long pool of Mulberry	18.25 × 25
Clarence Chapman (Mrs.)	Mulberry	undated	planting plan of bamboo garden	20.5 × 15.5
Clarence Chapman	Mulberry	11/241931	full-size detail for two post tops at Mulberry	23.5 × 20.75
Clarence Chapman	Mulberry	undated	full-size sketch: two Mulberry gatepost tops	21 × 25
Clarence Chapman (Mrs.)	Mulberry, Oakley, S.C.	6/15/1930	iron details	40.5 × 25
Historic Charleston Foundation	63 Laurens St. and 74 Anson St., Charleston	12/2/1966	construction plan foundation for gates and fence, walks, patio and steps	30.25 × 15
Historic Charleston Foundation	40-42-43 Society and 64-66-72 Anson, Charleston	6/24/1960	site plan for 40-42-43 Society and 64-66-72 Anson	29 × 17
Mr. and Mrs. Frederick Richards, Jr.	100 Tradd St., Charleston	undated	construction drawings— garden	19 × 26.5
Mr. and Mrs. James M. Hagood	23 Meeting St., Charleston	1/20/1970, and additions	construction plan of garden no. 1 and details	33.75 × 16.5
Mr. and Mrs. James M. Hagood	23 Meeting St., Charleston	2/2/1970, 3/12/1970, 5/30/1970, 5/22/1970	plan no. 2 for garden pool, sun dial base, grading, sunroom steps, irrigation	33/75 × 16.5
Mr. and Mrs. James M. Hagood	23 Meeting St., Charleston	4/21/1970	construction plan no. 3— tool house and lattice	27.5 × 19.75
Mr. and Mrs. James M. Hagood	23 Meeting St., Charleston	10/30/1965; notes added 11/3/1965	garden design	34.5 × 18
Mr. and Mrs. Rodney Williams	72 Anson St., Charleston	9/12/1970	construction and planting plan of grounds	23.5 × 17.75
Historic Charleston Foundation	Nathaniel Russell House, 51 Meeting St., Charleston	10/25/1967	proposed paving	26 × 12.7
Historic Charleston Foundation	Nathaniel Russell House, 51 Meeting St., Charleston	12/12/1969	completion of bases for four statues, walls and paving	26 × 12.75

CLIENT	NAME OF PROPERTY / ADDRESS	DATE(S) OF DRAWING(S)	TITLE	SIZE (W" × L")
Miss Sallie C. Carrington	7 Church St., Charleston	2/12/1965, rev'd 3/1/1965	Russell House garden construction plan—	16 × 27.5
Miss Sallie C. Carrington	7 Church St., Charleston	3/8/1948	plan of garden: preliminary print	23 × 30
Miss Sallie C. Carrington	7 Church St., Charleston	Undated	construction details— 1" = 1': garden pool	11 × 5.5

Selected Bibliography

Adams, Marty Whaley. "My Mother's Garden." *Southern Accents,* July–August 1989, 94–103.

American Society of Landscape Architects. *Illustration of Work of Members.* New York: House of J. Hayden Twiss, 1931.

———. *Illustration of Work of Members.* New York: House of J. Hayden Twiss, 1932.

———. *Illustration of Work of Members.* New York: House of J. Hayden Twiss, 1933.

"Architect Proposes City Beautification." *Charleston Post and Courier,* December 12, 1961.

Architectural League of New York. *Year Book of the Architectural League of New York.* New York: Press of Kalkhoff Company, 1931.

"Architecture: Modern in South Carolina." *House and Garden,* August 1937, 36–39.

Birnbaum, Charles A., and Robin Karson, eds. *Pioneers of American Landscape Design.* New York: McGraw-Hill, 2000.

Boisset, Caroline. *Town Gardens.* Boston: Little, Brown, 1989.

Briggs, Loutrel W. "Amateur Gardens—As Seen by a Landscape Architect." *Country Life,* 1930.

———. *Charleston Gardens.* Columbia: University of South Carolina Press, 1951.

———. "Charleston's Famous Gardens." *House and Garden,* March 1939, 45, 94–95.

———. "Fitting the Prize Offer House with a Garden." *Garden and Home Beautiful,* January 1926.

———. "Little Patterned Gardens of Old Charleston." *House and Garden,* May 1934.

———. "Planting for Our One Story Garden Home." *Garden and Home Beautiful,* May 1926.

———. "A Primer on Urban Renewal." *Charleston News and Courier,* April 12, 1964.

———. "The Roebling Garden." *House and Garden,* March 1933.

———. "Small House on the Little Lot." *Garden Magazine* 40 (January 1925).

Briggs, Loutrel W., and J. Floyd Yewell. "Your House and Its Grounds." *Garden and Home Beautiful,* January 1928, 46–47.

Bush, George S., ed. *The Genius Belt: The Story of the Arts in Bucks County, Pennsylvania.* University Park: James A. Michener Art Museum / Pennsylvania State University Press, 1996.

Cameron, Louisa Pringle. *The Charleston Gardner.* Charleston, S.C.: Wyrick, 2001.

———. *The Private Gardens of Charleston.* Charleston, S.C.: Wyrick, 1992.

Cothran, James R. *Gardens and Historic Plants of the Antebellum South.* Columbia: University of South Carolina Press, 2003.

———. *Gardens of Historic Charleston.* Columbia: University of South Carolina Press, 1995.

———. "Lasting Impressions: The Legacy of Landscape Architect Loutrel Briggs." *Charleston Magazine,* April 2004, 104–10.

Davis, Evangeline. *Charleston: Houses and Gardens.* Charleston, S.C.: Preservation Society of Charleston, 1975.

Derieux, James C. "The Renaissance of the Plantation." *Country Life,* January 1932, 34–39.

Duncan, Frances. "Charleston Gardens." *Century Magazine,* March 1907, 705–19.

Fleitmann, Dorothy. "Mrs. Washington Robling's House at Charleston." *Town and Country* 87 (January 15, 1933): 20–25.

Graydon, Nell S. *South Carolina Gardens.* Beaufort, S.C.: Beaufort Book Co., 1973.

Griswold, Mac, and Eleanor Weller. *The Golden Age of American Gardens: Proud Owners, Private Estates, 1890–1940.* New York: Abrams / Garden Club of America. 1991.

Hunt, Stephanie. "The Renaissance Revival: An Enduring Legacy." *Charleston Magazine,* supplement (November 2002).

Hutchisson, James M., and Harlan Greene, eds. *Renaissance in Charleston: Art and Life in the Carolina Low Country, 1900–1940.* Athens: University of Georgia Press, 2003.

Lockwood, Alice G. B., ed. *Gardens of Colony and State: Gardens and Gardeners of the American Colonies and of the Republic before 1840.* Vol. 2. New York: Scribners for the Garden Club of America,

1934. Reprint, New York: Smallwood & Stewart for the Garden Club of America, 2000.

"Mepkin Plantation, Moncks Corner, S.C.: Winter Home for Mr. and Mrs. Henry Luce." *Architectural Forum* 66 (June 1937): 515–22.

Odenwald, Neil G., and James R. Turner. *Identification Selection for Use of Southern Plants for Landscape Design.* Baton Rouge: Clairot's Press, 1987.

Ohrbach, Barbara Milo. "Charleston in Full Bloom." *Southern Accents,* March–April 1996, 170–77.

Poston, Jonathan H. *The Buildings of Charleston: A Guide to the City's Architecture.* Columbia: University of South Carolina Press, 1997.

Prewitt, Karen. "Loutrel Briggs: Charleston's Premiere Landscape Architect." *Carologue* 9 (Spring 1993): 22–24.

———. "Save Our Gardens." *Charleston Horticultural Society Bulletin,* Spring 2001.

Ravenel, Harriott Horry (Rutledge). "Mrs. St. Julien Ravenel." In *Charleston, the Place and the People.* New York: Macmillan, 1906.

Reisman, Eric. "The Use of Conservation Easements to Protect Gardens of Cultural and Historic Significance." Master's thesis, University of Georgia, 2009.

Richardson, Emma B. *Charleston Garden Plats.* Charleston Museum leaflet no. 19. Charleston, S.C.: Charleston Museum, 1943.

———. *The Heyward-Washington House Garden.* Charleston Museum leaflet no. 15. Charleston, S.C.: Charleston Museum, 1941.

Saunders, Boyd, and Ann McAden. *Alfred Hutty and the Charleston Renaissance.* Orangeburg, S.C.: Sandlapper Publishing, 1990.

Severens, Martha R. *The Charleston Renaissance.* Spartanburg, S.C.: Saraland Press, 1998.

———. "The Charleston Renaissance." *Carologue* 14 (Autumn 1998): 16–21.

Shaffer, Edward Terry Hendrie. *Carolina Gardens.* Chapel Hill: University of North Carolina Press, 1939.

Southern Garden History Society. *Magnolia* 1– (1984–).

"Spirit of Old Charleston." *House Beautiful,* January 1936.

Verey, Rosemary. "The Walled Gardens of Charleston." *Horticulture,* April 1998, 40–48.

Verey, Rosemary, and Ellen Samuels. *The American Woman's Garden.* Boston: Little, Brown, 1984.

Wedda, John. *Gardens of the American South.* New York: Galahad, 1971.

Weyeneth, Robert R. *Historic Preservation for a Living City: Historic Charleston Foundation 1947–1997.* Columbia: University of South Carolina Press, 2000.

Whaley, Emily, in conversation with William Baldwin. *Mrs. Whaley and Her Charleston Garden.* Chapel Hill, N.C.: Algonquin Books of Chapel Hill, 1997.

"William Gibbes House, Charleston, S.C., Mrs. W. A. Roebling, Owner." *American Architect and Architecture,* June 1936, 43–53.

Willis, Eola. "Catfish Row Comes Back." *Country Life,* April 1930, 49–51.

Wood, Ernest. "Charleston: A Walk with History." *Southern Living,* March 1988, 104–7.

Yuhl, Stephanie E. *A Golden Haze of Memory: The Making of Historic Charleston.* Chapel Hill: University of North Carolina Press, 2005.

Index

Illustration Credits

Pages 68–69. Photographs by Alexander Wallace

Page 70. Photograph by the author

Page 71. Author's collection

Page 72. Photographs by the author

Page 74. Photograph by David Dozier

Page 75. Drawing by Loutrel Briggs. Courtesy of Historic Charleston Foundation

Pages 76–79. Photographs by the author

Pages 80–87 (top). Photographs by the author

Page 87 (bottom). Photograph by David Dozier

Pages 88–105, 108, 115. Photographs by the author

Page 116 (left). Courtesy of HALS—Historic American Landscapes Survey, National Park Services Brochure

Page 116 (right). Photograph by the author

Page 118. Author's collection

About the Author

James R. Cothran is a practicing landscape architect, urban planner, and garden historian in Atlanta. He holds degrees from Clemson University, the University of Georgia, and the Georgia Institute of Technology. Cothran serves as an adjunct professor at the University of Georgia and Georgia State University, where he teaches graduate courses on America's historic gardens and landscapes. A fellow in the American Society of Landscape Architects, Cothran is past president of the Southern Garden History Society and currently serves on the boards of the Alliance for Historic Landscape Preservation, Trees Atlanta, and the Cherokee Garden Library–Center for the Study of Southern Garden History. He is the author of *Gardens of Historic Charleston* and *Gardens and Historic Plants of the Antebellum South,* which has been honored with awards from the American Society of Landscape Architects, the National Garden Clubs, the Council on Botanical and Horticultural Libraries, the Georgia Historical Society, and other organizations.